The Evolution of

# NORTH AMERICAN INDIANS

*A
31-volume
series of
outstanding
dissertations*

*Edited by*
DAVID HURST THOMAS
American Museum of Natural History

A GARLAND SERIES

# THE EVOLUTION OF NORTH AMERICAN INDIANS

# Spanish-Indian Relations in Florida

## A Study of Two Visitas, 1657–1678

### FRED LAMAR PEARSON, JR.

Garland Publishing, Inc.    New York & London    1990

Library of Congress Cataloging-in-Publication Data

Pearson, Fred Lamar.
Spanish-Indian relations in Florida : a study of two visitas, 1657–1678 / Fred
Lamar Pearson, Jr.
p. cm. — (The Evolution of North American Indians)
Includes bibliographical references (p.  ).
ISBN 0-8240-2510-5 (alk. paper)
1. Indians of North America—Florida—Government relations. 2. Indians of
North America—Florida—History—17th century. 3. Indians of North
America—Florida—Social life and customs. 4. Colonial administrators—
Florida. 5. Spain—Colonies—America. I. Title. II. Series.
E78.F6P43               1990
975.9'00497—dc20        90-14048

Printed on acid-free, 250-year-life paper.
Manufactured in the United States of America.

Design by J. Threlkeld

## PREFACE

The Spanish government used the visita or investigation for a number of reasons. Basically, it was an attempt whereby both specific and general information was obtained. On the basis of this data both immediate and long range policies could be formulated. The value of the study depended, of course, on the individual who conducted it.

Governor Rebolledo's investigation in 1657, although it revealed a good deal of data, pales when placed beside the investigations of Arguelles and Leturiondo. This becomes apparent when one takes a closer look at the evidence. The probability that he used his investigation to cover up the inadequacies of his administration--especially that part which related to Indian policy--is high. The fact that the Council of the Indies removed him from office lends substance to the probability.

The visitadors sent out by Governor Hita Salazar had no vested interest to protect. There had been no

i

Indian problems such as the Timucuan rebellion which faced Rebolledo. As a result, Arguelles' and Leturiondo's report reflect an in-depth study of the pueblo society, its multi-component parts, and Spanish relations to it.

Throughout the dissertation words such as cacique, enija, visitador, visita, etc., appear. No attempt has been made to underline them, for they have all appeared countless times in the periodical and monographic literature.

## ACKNOWLEDGMENTS

The preparation of this dissertation has indebted me to several individuals. First, I should like to acknowledge my appreciation to Dr. Lewis W. Wetzler, my director. His guidance, friendship, and interest in the study are sincerely appreciated.

Dr. Edward Moseley, the second reader, certainly broadened the scope of the dissertation. His critical comments and sage advice went far to improve the study.

A word of appreciation is also due to Dr. Paul Nesbitt of the Anthropology Department who served as the third reader.

An especial gratitude is due my parents whose financial assistance and unfailing interest went far to make this dissertation a reality.

I can never express adequately my appreciation to Nancy Page Pearson. Her devotion and interest in things academic never flagged throughout.

TABLE OF CONTENTS

CHAPTER I

THE STRUCTURE OF INDIAN SOCIETY AND

EARLY SPANISH CONTACT TO 1565

Man entered the western hemisphere probably as
early as 35,000 years ago. The origin of this aboriginee
is not known for certain. Most authorities accept the
theory that the immigrant originated somewhere in central
Asia. Bands of these early men moved northward to Siberia
following migrating herds of animals from which they de-
rived most of their food. Once in Siberia, early man
found that conditions were opportune, between 25,000 and
10,000 years ago, to permit him to cross the Bering Strait
into the western hemisphere. During this period great Ice
Ages occurred which lowered the level of the oceans and
sometimes exposed a land mass connecting Asia to North
America. It is possible the aboriginee crossed into
Alaska via the ice mass in winter as the Eskimo does to-
day. In any event Paleo or early man arrived in the
hemisphere at an early date, and he moved slowly

throughout the two continents and the Caribbean Islands.

By approximately 8,000 years ago Paleo Man had reached

Tierra del Fuego at the tip of South America. Sites in

the west date 20,000 or more years ago, and Carbon 14

dates for the Lewisville site in Texas may exceed 35,000

years ago, although the accuracy of this date has been

questioned. In any event, the large number of Indian dia-

lects that have developed in the hemisphere and the Carbon

14 dates obtained indicate a considerable antiquity for

the aboriginee.[1]

These people, misnamed Indians by Columbus, settled

along streams and lakes. In Spanish Florida[2] Indian

groups such as the Guale, Timucua, Apalachee, Edisto,

Apalachicola, Chatot, and Westoes lived in geographical

---

[1]Kenneth Macgowan, Early Man in the New World (New York: The Macmillan Company, 1950); Gordon R. Willey and Philip Phillips, Method and Theory in American Archaeology (Chicago: The University of Chicago Press, 1958), p. 87; David L. DeJarnette, Edward B. Kurjack, and James W. Cambron, "Stanfield-Worley Bluff Shelter Excavations," Journal of Alabama Archaeology, VII (June, December, 1962), p. 1, hereinafter cited as J.A.A.

[2]Spanish Florida constituted a vaguely defined region which extended from the Keys to Labrador along the Atlantic coast. The boundary to the west had no precise limits.

locations that can be roughly defined. The Guale Indians
lived along the Georgia coast and on the off-shore islands.
Guale province extended approximately from the Savannah
River on the north to the area of St. Andrews Sound to the
south.[3] The width of the province is difficult to determine. Probably Guale extended no further into the interior of the Georgia country than a few miles. Timucua
province can be defined with even less accuracy than
Guale, for the north and south boundaries are difficult
to ascertain. Possibly the province included Cumberland
Island to the north, and it extended a few miles south of
St. Augustine. The western boundary of the province was
the Aucilla River. Geographically, Timucua had its
principal concentration of population near the Lake Santa
Fé region. The province protruded partially into Georgia;
in western Florida it extended possibly as far south as
Tampa Bay.[4] Apalachee province, further to the west,

---

[3] John R. Swanton, Early History of the Creek Indians and Their Neighbors (Washington: Bureau of American
Ethnology, Bulletin 73, 1922), p. 80, hereinafter cited
as Early History of the Creek Indians.

[4] David I. Bushnell, Jr., Native Villages and Village Sites East of the Mississippi (Washington: Bureau

centered around present-day Tallahassee. It was limited
principally by the Aucilla River on the east and by the
Ocklocknee River and its tributaries to the west. The
principal settlement of the Edisto Indians was about five
or six leagues north of Santa Elena or Port Royal, South
Carolina.[5] The Apalachicolas, the name which the Spanish
gave to the Lower Creeks, lived along the Chattanoochee
River. Their greatest concentration of villages was near
present-day Columbus, Georgia.[6] Near the Apalachicola
River, the Chatot Indians lived. Actually their settlements were located on the western side of the river "near
the middle course of the Chipola."[7] The Westoes lived on
the Savannah River below Augusta, Georgia.[8] Over a number
of centuries these Indian groups developed a society which
embraced several social levels.

---

of American Ethnology, Bulletin 69, 1919), pp. 15, 89.
See also Swanton, Early History of the Creek Indians, pp.
320-330.

[5]Swanton, Early History of the Creek Indians, pp.
60-61.

[6]Ibid., pp. 129-131.

[7]Ibid., p. 134.

[8]Ibid., p. 306.

The principal official in the Indian village was the cacique or chief. In Guale province the term mico was used more often than cacique. Sometimes in Spanish documents one sees the term tunaque which referred to a cacique also. Generally the chief's jurisdiction extended no further than the geographical limits of the village in which he lived. Sometimes, however, the cacique exercised suzerainty over several towns, and in Guale there was, from time to time, a sort of head mico to whom the other micos rendered a degree of obeisance. An Indian ascended to the caciqueship through matrilinear succession as a general rule, but deviations from this practice took place when there was no heredero or heir to succeed to the office. In this case the caciqueship descended to a nephew or close relative, or the Spanish officials conferred the title on an esteemed Indian after having ascertained the sentiments of the villagers. Not infrequently the pueblo cacique renounced his position prior to his demise and the legitimate heir assumed the position. Men, as a rule, exercised the position, but sometimes women served as the village rulers. The cacique exerted more power and influence in the Indian town than any other individual.[9]

The cacique sought the advice of subordinate officials in the village before he made an important decision. Collectively, the Spaniards knew these individuals
as principal men. Of these principal men, the enija exerted considerable influence in tribal affairs. Enijas
acted as companions, seconds, or lieutenants of the
chiefs, and during the Green Corn Dance, an enija accompanied each principal official. The enija had charge
of purification rites such as the "Black Drink" ceremony
which the Indians observed widely throughout the southeast. This drink or beverage was prepared from the holly

---

[9]John R. Swanton, Social Organization and Social
Usages of the Indians of the Creek Confederacy (Washing-
ton: Bureau of American Ethnology, Forty-Second Annual
Report, 1928), pp. 114, 277, 306, hereinafter cited as
Social Organization and Social Usages; Swanton, Early
History of the Creek Indians, p. 84; Theodore H. Lewis
(ed.), "The Narrative of the Expedition of Hernando de
Soto, by the Gentleman of Elvas," in J. Franklin Jameson
(ed.), Spanish Explorers in the Southern United States,
1528-1543 in Original Narratives of American History (New
York: Barnes and Noble Reprint, 1959), p. 164, herein-
after cited as Spanish Explorers; Auto [San Francisco de
Potano], January 24, 1678, John B. Stetson Collection,
Escribanía de Camara, Legajo 156, p. 609, hereinafter
cited as Stet. Coll. Escrib. de Cam., Leg.; Vicita del
lugar de San Joseph de Sapala, December 24, 1677, Stet.
Coll. Escrib. de Cam., Leg. 156, pp. 526-527.

plant. The Indians drank the brew in order to appease
the spirits both beneficent and malevolent. As such, the
drink played a conspicuous role in their highly ceremonial
social system. The enija played a role secondary only to
that of the cacique.[10]

The principal men acted as a council of elders,
serving as advisors to caciques when needed, and it appears that some of them were even caciques themselves.
The Gentleman of Elvas wrote with respect to the principal man that the

> . . . cacique came out to receive him [de Soto] at
> the distance of two crossbow-shot from the town,
> borne in a litter on the shoulders of his princi-
> pal men, seated on a cushion, and covered with a
> mantle of marten-skins, of the size and shape of
> a woman's shawl: on his head he wore a diadem of

---

[10] Swanton, Social Organization and Social Usages,
pp. 192-195. See also Benjamin Hawkins, "A Sketch of the
Creek Country in the Years 1798 and 1799," in Collections
of the Georgia Historical Society, III (Savannah: 1848),
69. The Indians brewed the leaves of the holly (ilex
vomitorio) tree to make the Black Drink. This drink produced nausea when the Indians consumed it, and they used
it as an emetic on ceremonial occasions. At the Ockmul-
gee State Park at Macon, Georgia, one can see special
holes constructed in the earth lodge which served as re-
ceptacles. How an Indian could have gone into battle or
played the ball game after consuming such a vile drink is
difficult to imagine.

plumes, and he was surrounded by many attendants
playing upon flutes and singing.[11]

The term "principal men" is vague, and it appears that
the Spaniards used it sometimes to classify a group of
important Indians who ranked somewhere beneath the
cacique.[12]

The role of the mandador is not clear.  Probably
the term referred to a person who served as a principal
man.[13]  Warriors served possibly as principal men.  Re-
nown braves enjoyed a good deal of prestige in the village; probably they advanced up the social ladder as a
result of their military prowess.[14]

The medicine man exercised an important role in

---

[11]Lewis (ed.), "The Narrative of the Expedition of
Hernando de Soto, by the Gentleman of Elvas," Spanish Explorers, p. 183.

[12]See Vicita de San Damían de Cupaica, January 17,
1657, Stet. Coll. Escrib. de Cam., Leg. 155, pp. 2-3;
Vicita del lugar [Santa María] de Bacuqua, January 19,
1657, Stet. Coll. Escrib. de Cam., Leg. 155, pp. 7-10;
Vicita del lugar de San Pedro [de] Patali, January 19,
1657, Stet. Coll. Escrib. de Cam., Leg. 155, p. 10.

[13]Titulo de 29 de Noviembre por la descargo, Stet.
Coll. Escrib. de Cam., Leg. 156, pp. 520-521.

[14]Swanton, Early History of the Creek Indians, pp.
376-380.

tribal life. He served as a priest and as a doctor.
Women sometimes served as shamans, commanding the same
respect. These medicine men treated diseases, served as
rain makers, prepared curses and love potions and a host
of other spells and incantations. Because of his knowledge, the shaman exercised power which rivaled that of
the cacique. When the Spanish priest came to Florida,
his interest and that of the shaman came into direct conflict. While their medical knowledge was scant, medicine
men knew a great deal about botany. While recognizing
the medicinal value of many herbs, the medicine man did
not cultivate them himself. He preferred to gather them
in their natural habitat. Perhaps two of his most important functions related to the ball game and war. When
the Indians departed to play a game, he, rather than the
cacique, gave them a pep talk, and he accompanied the
Indians when they went to war.[15]

---

[15] James Mooney, The Swimmer Manuscript: Cherokee
Sacred Formulas and Medicinal Prescriptions, Revised, Com-
piled, and Edited by Frans M. Olbrechts (Washington:
Bureau of American Ethnology, Bulletin 99, 1932), pp. 18-
123. See also Swanton, Early History of the Creek Indians,
pp. 45, 56, 79, 385; John R. Swanton, Religious Beliefs
and Medical Practices of the Creek Indians (Washington:

Not only did the southeastern Indians possess a complex society, but they had also a rich cultural complex. They worshipped many gods, and religion played an important role in every facet of their lives. Before the Indians played the ball game or went to war, they engaged in various rituals to prepare themselves for the contests. When the Indians enjoyed success on the hunt, they offered a part of the game as a sacrifice. They believed in totemism and hence did not kill animals which represented their clan totem. Certain parts of the animals were not eaten because of taboos. A hunter did not eat the tail of a deer for fear that he could not get close enough to another animal to affect a kill. Indian burial customs reflected interesting variations also. Near Tampa, Cabeza de Vaca, a member of the Narváez expedition saw Timucuan corpses enclosed in wooden cases and covered with painted deer skins, and Juan Ortíz, a survivor of the Narváez expedition rescued by de Soto, served for a time as a temple watcher so that animals did not carry off the

Bureau of American Ethnology, Forty-Second Annual Report, 1928), pp. 475-672, hereinafter cited as Religious Beliefs and Medical Practices.

bodies at night. Here these bodies stayed until they had
decomposed. An individual, known as the Buzzard Man,
scraped the residual flesh from the bones and placed them
in a mortuary house. In other areas the Indians interred
the body along with possessions which the deceased esteemed. Sometimes the Indians practiced secondary buri-
als, and mutilation of the bodies was not infrequent.[16]

The Indian town or village consisted of a number of
dwellings constructed usually of logs with roofs made of
straw, palmetto leaves, and cane. The Indians sharpened
logs and put them vertically into the ground. They wove
vines through the logs to make a mat. On top of this mat,
they caked wet clay to close the holes and cracks in the
walls. This type of construction is known as wattle and
daub. Each dwelling contained an aperture in the roof to
permit the smoke to escape. There was a difference

---

[16] James Mooney, The Swimmer Manuscript: Cherokee
Sacred Formulas and Medicinal Prescriptions, pp. 91-92;
John R. Swanton, Aboriginal Culture of the Southeast
(Washington: Bureau of American Ethnology, Forty-Second
Annual Report, 1928), pp. 700-701; Swanton, Religious Be-
liefs and Medical Practices, pp. 517-521; Lewis (ed.),
"The Narrative of the Expedition of Hernando de Soto, by
the Gentleman of Elvas," Spanish Explorers, p. 150;
Frederick W. Hodge (ed.), "The Narrative of Alvar Núñez
Cabeca de Vaca," Spanish Explorers, p. 21.

between the dwellings of the important people of the village and those of the common individuals.  The Gentleman
of Elvas said:

> . . . The difference between the houses of the
> masters, or principal men, and those of the com-
> mon people is that, besides being larger than the
> others, they have deep balconies on the front
> side, with cane seats, like benches and about are
> many barbacoas, in which they bring together the
> tribute their people give them of maize skins, of
> deer, and blankets of the country.[17]

Often times the Indians had winter and summer houses.  In
Apalachee, the natives constructed their homes low to the
ground to minimize the destructiveness of the hurricanes
which passed through the area with a disconcerting frequency.[18]  In addition to dwelling houses the Indians had
other structures which served utilitarian purposes.

The barbacoa or storage house was used to store

---

[17]Lewis (ed.), "The Narrative of the Expedition of
Hernando de Soto, by the Gentleman of Elvas," Spanish Explorers, p. 165.

[18]Lewis (ed.), "The Narrative of the Expedition of
Hernando de Soto, by the Gentleman of Elvas," Spanish Explorers, pp. 147, 165, 187; Bushnell, Native Villages and
Village Sites, pp. 83-89; Swanton, Early History of the
Creek Indians, pp. 352-353; Hodge (ed.), "The Narrative
of Alvar Núñez Cabeca de Vaca," Spanish Explorers, p.
28.

food.  The Gentleman of Elvas writes that ". . . Maize is

kept in a barbacoa, which is a house with wooden sides,

like a room, raised aloft on four posts, and has a floor

of cane."[19]  Buhíos, or council houses, were large com-

munal structures where the Indians gathered for tribal

conferences and festive gatherings.  Cabeza de Vaca esti-

mated that a council house he saw had sufficient space to

accommodate three hundred individuals.[20]  These Indian

structures were short-lived for the materials used in

their construction decomposed rapidly.  Because of the

simplicity of design and construction, the Indian could

replace his home without difficulty.

Outside of the housing perimeter, the Indians had

agricultural plots where they cultivated food crops such

as beans, maize, squash, and calabashes.  Prior to the

arrival of Europeans in the southeastern United States,

agriculture constituted the Indian's primary source of

---

[19]Lewis (ed.), "The Narrative of the Expedition of
Hernando de Soto, by the Gentleman of Elvas," Spanish Explorers, p. 165.

[20]Lewis (ed.), "The Narrative of the Expedition of
Hernando de Soto, by the Gentleman of Elvas," Spanish Ex-
plorers, p. 165; Hodge (ed.), "The Narrative of Alvar
Núñez Cabeca de Vaca," Spanish Explorers, p. 19.

subsistence. Although the Indians had a simple type of
farming technology, when compared with modern techniques,
the yield which they obtained permitted the development
of significant towns and cultural centers. Some of these
towns, such as that at Moundville, Alabama, grew to a considerable size. The influence of such cultural centers
extended far beyond the geographical boundaries of the
town. Indians from surrounding areas came to these
centers from time to time to trade with each other, to
play the ball game, and to perform ceremonial dances.[21]

The Indian ball game, played widely throughout the
Americas, was a very rough and dangerous sport. When the
Indians wanted to play a game with a neighboring village,
they dispatched a messenger to the town which they had
challenged. This envoy worked out the exact date for the
game and the number of participants to represent each
town. Generally between forty and fifty players from
each town took part in the game. The Apalachee Indians
played the game at either midday or early afternoon in

[21]Douglas H. McKenzie, "A Summary of the Moundville
Phase," J.A.A., XII (June, 1966), 1-55; Willey and
Phillips, Method and Theory in American Archaeology, p.
165.

summer months. The Indians wore only a breech cloth on the field. They tied their hair in a knot and adorned their bodies with various colors of paint. Some of them painted their faces red and their bodies black, while other players displayed red streaks on their bodies. As such they represented various animals such as the wolf, bear, panther, stag, and fox.[22]

The contest began when a principal man threw a ball made of stuffed deer skin into the middle of the players. This caused a vigorous struggle as the teams fought to gain possession of the ball. Frequently a pile-up occurred as the opponents fell in their efforts to obtain it. Players struggled vigorously to free themselves and to put the ball into play. The team which gained possession of the ball kicked it toward the opponent's goal. Each team attempted to kick the ball into an elevated goal, and the side which accomplished this feat eleven times won the game.[23]

---

[22]"Description of the Indian Ball Game," by Diego de Salvador and Juan de Mendoza, September 3, 1676, Stet. Coll. Escrib. de Cam., Leg. 156, pp. 568-583.

[23]Ibid.

Because of the pile-ups which occurred frequently
in the game, players sometimes received serious injuries.
Often four or five of the Indians lay stretched out on the
ground in an unconscious state. Indians, who had their
mouths crammed full of dirt, fought desperately to catch
their breath, while others displayed signs of nausea, because they received blows to the stomach and had their
windpipes crushed. A few players suffered broken arms and
legs. After the game concluded, the players not physically incapacitated revived themselves by pouring buckets
of water over their bodies. Because the game was so
rough, the Spanish suspended it.[24]

Spain moved northward from her Caribbean Island
bases early in the sixteenth century in an effort to explore the North American coast line and interior. The
conquistadors left Spain and the Caribbean settlements to
penetrate the wild interior of the North American continent for several reasons. The prospect of finding gold,
silver, and precious stones was a major motive. The River
Jordon and the Fountain of Youth were thought to be

---

[24] Ibid.

somewhere to the north, and more than one expedition set out in search of them. The desire to propagate the Catholic faith exercised influence on the explorers who came to Florida, but no priest accompanied the first Spanish expedition to Florida in 1513.[25]

Juan Ponce de León, the conqueror of Puerto Rico, heard the Indian legend of an island to the north which possessed a marvelous fountain. Supposedly, he who bathed in its water would be physically rejuvenated. Anxious to find such a place, León appealed to the crown to obtain permission to go in search of the island called Bimini. On February 23, 1512, León received permission to lead an expedition at his own expense in quest of the island. The crown conferred on him the title, adelantado, and instructed him to distribute to members of the expedition any Indians that he encountered. León, from his own funds, outfitted three vessels and departed from San Germán, Puerto Rico, March 3, 1513. In early April, the expedition sighted the Florida Peninsula. The beautiful

---

[25]Michael V. Gannon, The Cross in the Sand: The Early Catholic Church in Florida 1513-1870 (Gainesville: University of Florida Press, 1965), p. 2.

flora of the coast so impressed the adelantado that he
named the area Florida.  Noticing inhabitants on the
shore, the Spanish landed, and the Indians attacked them.
The León expedition sailed up both sides of the peninsula
noting geographical landmarks on the way.  Cape Cañaveral
(plantation of reeds or canes), recently renamed Cape
Kennedy, received from León the name, Cabo de las Cor-
rientes, and he called the Florida Keys, Los Martires.
The expedition spent most of the summer of 1513 recon-
noitering the coastal area, and León returned to Puerto
Rico in September.[26]

Although Ponce de León obtained a second patent
September 27, 1514, which authorized him to go again to
Florida to establish a colony, a number of years passed
before he returned.  During his absence, three other
Spaniards touched on the peninsula.  Diego Miruelo sailed
from Cuba to Florida in 1516 where he traded with the
Indians, and he obtained supposedly some gold trinkets

---

[26]Woodbury Lowery, The Spanish Settlements within
the Present Limits of the United States 1513-1561 (New
York:  Russell and Russell, Inc., Reprint, 1959), I,
134-143, hereinafter cited as The Spanish Settlements.

in return for his trade goods.[27] The following year,

1517, Francisco Fernández de Córdoba landed on the Florida

coast. His expedition, which sailed first to the Yucatan

Peninsula, encountered rough weather on the return voyage

to Cuba. The chief pilot, Anton de Alimanos, who had ac-

companied León's expedition, prevailed on Córdoba to land

on the Florida coast for repairs and to replenish water

supplies. Several Spaniards went ashore where they found

the Indians hostile. The Indians wounded a number of the

soldiers, including Captain Córdoba and Bernal Díaz del

Castillo. The expedition returned to Cuba where Captain

Córdoba died from his wounds.[28] Alonso Alvárez de Pineda

led the fourth Spanish expedition to Florida. Pineda com-

manded four vessels which Governor Francisco de Garay of

Jamaica outfitted. He sailed from the Tampico region of

Mexico to the tip of the Florida peninsula. Pineda found,

---

[27] Anthony Kerrigan (trans.), _Barcia's Chronological History of the Continent of Florida from the Year 1512, in which Ponce de Leon Discovered Florida, Until the Year 1722_ (Gainesville: University of Florida Press, 1954), p. 3.

[28] Ibid.; J. M. Cohen (trans.), _Bernal Díaz, The Conquest of New Spain_ (Baltimore: Penquin Books, Reprint, 1965), pp. 25-26.

along the Gulf Coast, the mouth of a large river, on both
banks of which stood several Indian villages. The dispute
as to whether this river was the Mississippi or the Mobile
has not been settled.[29] Alonso Pineda's expedition proved
conclusively that Florida was not an island but part of
the mainland. Also important is the fact that Pineda's
expedition completed the charting of the Gulf Coast for
Spain.[30]

Ponce de León sailed again for Florida soon after
Pineda completed his voyage. The adelantado carried with
him colonists, agricultural tools, seeds, and animals to
establish a settlement. Catholic missionaries accompanied
León, for the 1514 patent instructed him to begin missionary work among the Indians he encountered. The crown
empowered him to enslave the Indians if they proved un-
receptive to the Christian religion. León landed on the
west coast of the Florida peninsula near Charlotte Harbor.

---

[29]Swanton, Early History of the Creek Indians, pp.
150-151. Swanton is of the opinion that this was the
Mobile River rather than the Mississippi because of
numerous Indian sites around the mouth of the Mobile
River and the dearth of sites around the mouth of the
Mississippi River.

[30]Lowery, Spanish Settlements, I, 149-151.

He led his followers ashore to establish a colony, but he
encountered Indian hostility which forced him to abandon
his plans. Several members of the expedition met their
death in a skirmish with the Indians, and León, wounded
badly, died soon after returning to Cuba.[31]

While Juan Ponce de León had tried without success
to establish a settlement in Florida, other Spanish entre-
preneurs in the Caribbean focused their attention on the
peninsula to the north. One such Spaniard was Lucas
Vázquez de Ayllón. A Knight of the Order of Santiago and
a lawyer by training, Ayllón advanced quickly in the
Spanish civil service, and the crown made him a member
of the audiencia of Santo Domingo.[32] Ayllón heard ac-
counts of a land mass north of the Bahama Island chain.
Interested in confirming the report, Ayllón equipped a
vessel and dispatched it on a reconnaissance mission under

[31]Ibid., pp. 158-159.

[32]Paul Quattlebaum, The Land Called Chicora: The
Carolinas under Spanish Rule with French Intrusions 1520-
1670 (Gainesville: University of Florida Press, 1956),
pp. 4-5, hereinafter cited as The Land Called Chicora.
See also J. G. Johnson, "A Spanish Settlement in Carolina,
1526," Georgia Historical Quarterly, VII (December, 1923),
338-341, hereinafter cited as G.H.Q.

the command of Francisco Gordillo.  Although Ayllón was a
slave owner, he ordered Gordillo to capture no Indians on
his voyage.  Gordillo sailed north along the Atlantic sea-
board and made many landings, especially in the Carolinas,
called Chicora by the Spaniards.  He encountered a vessel
commanded by Pedro de Quexos while in the area.  Quexos
persuaded Gordillo to join him in a slave hunt, and he
violated Ayllón's instructions.  The commanders loaded
their ships with a human cargo and returned to Santo
Domingo to sell the Indians into slavery.[33]  Ayllón,
angered that Gordillo had disobeyed his orders, carried
the matter before Governor Diego Columbus who ordered
the Indians returned to their homes.[34]

Ayllón traveled to Spain seeking permission to
colonize Chicora.  He took Francisco Chicorano, a Chicora
Indian, with him to bolster his pretensions to the area.
Chicorano entertained the Spanish court with stories of a

---

[33]The encomienda was a grant of Indians to a
Spaniard to use as a labor force.  The Spaniards did not
own the Indians but merely had them entrusted to their
care.  See Lesley Byrd Simpson, The Encomienda in New
Spain; The Beginning of Spanish Mexico (Berkeley:  University of California Press, New Edition, 1950).

[34]Quattlebaum, The Land Called Chicora, pp. 7-13.

giant King Datha and of inhabitants of the region who had tails. King Charles I, impressed with Ayllón's plans for the area, granted a patent June 12, 1523, which authorized him to establish a colony in the Carolinas. Official duties prevented Ayllón from setting out to colonize the area until 1526. During the interim, Quexos returned the captured Indians to their homes. In July, 1526, Governor Ayllón departed with his colonizing expedition, which included several hundred men and women. The Spaniards landed probably at Cape Fear which they called the River Jordan. Ayllón lost a vessel in landing, and Chicorano fled to his aboriginal friends. Unimpressed by the Cape Fear area, Ayllón sailed down the Carolina coast where he established a settlement, San Miguel de Gualdape, on the Waccamaw River.[35] Misfortune plagued the settlement almost from the start. Disease struck the inhabitants and several of the colonists died including Ayllón. A mutiny occurred because the colony lacked effective leadership after Ayllón's death. The harsh winter that came thoroughly discouraged the remaining settlers, and the

[35]Ibid., pp. 15-23.

colonists decided to abandon San Miguel and return to
Hispaniola.[36]

Panfilo de Narváez, who rendered signal service to
Governor Diego de Velázquez in the conquest of Cuba, was
the next conquistador to lead an expedition to Florida.
The crown appointed Narváez as governor of Florida because
of his distinguished service record. Narváez, with an expedition of approximately five hundred colonists, sailed
from Spain to the Caribbean in 1527, but he did not touch
on the Florida peninsula until April, 1528. Alvar Núñez
Cabeza de Vaca accompanied Narváez and served as treasurer
and high-sheriff. Narváez landed April 14, 1528, "somewhere in the vicinity of St. Clements Point on the peninsula west of Tampa Bay."[37]  Here, the Spaniards encountered the Timucuan Indians. Governor Narváez asked
de Vaca to assume command of the fleet while he led most
of the expedition northward on land. The governor planned
to rendezvous with the ships in a harbor large enough to
accommodate them securely. He intended, after securing

[36]Ibid., pp. 24-27.

[37]Lowery, Spanish Settlements, I, 177.

the fleet, to explore the interior extensively. Cabeza de
Vaca declined the command, and Narváez appointed an official named Caravallo to the position. Having selected
a fleet commander, Narváez moved into the interior and
headed toward Apalachee province. When he arrived at
Aute, located near St. Marks,[38] he learned that no fleet
awaited him on the coast. The expedition faced a serious
food shortage and casualties from Indian attacks had
weakened it considerably. Narváez, well aware of his
precarious situation, decided to construct vessels out
of available material in a frantic effort to reach Mexico.
The soldiers gave up their stirrups, spurs, and other
metal objects which they melted to make nails. They constructed five boats of dubious stability. De Vaca and
his fellow soldiers made ropes from palm trees and from
the tails and manes of the horses. The men used their
shirts to make sails. They placed as much food and water
as possible in the fragile crafts, and the Narváez expedition set out for Mexico skirting the coastline. The

---

[38] Hodge (ed.), "The Narrative of Alvar Núñez Cabeza
de Vaca," Spanish Explorers, p. 30.

Spaniards endured inadequate food and water and inclement weather a large part of the time. Separated from Narváez, de Vaca forged ahead to Malhado Island[39] where his boat wrecked. He learned there that Narváez had been lost on the gulf.[40] Most of the expedition force perished but Cabeza de Vaca and three companions[41] succeeded in reaching Culiacán, New Spain, after a perilous journey across the southwest which took eight years.

De Vaca, soon after reaching Mexico, journeyed to Spain where he petitioned the crown to confer upon him the governorship of Florida. He arrived too late, for Don Hernando de Soto had already received the title. De Soto, who had served under Francisco de Pizarro in Peru, asked de Vaca to accompany him to Florida, but he declined. On May 18, 1539, de Soto departed from Havana, and landed May 30 at Ucita.[42] A scouting party dispatched into the

---

[39] Ibid., pp. 48-49.

[40] Ibid., pp. 33-62.

[41] The three were Alonso del Castillo Maldonado, Andrés Dorantes, and Estevanico.

[42] Lewis (ed.), "The Narrative of the Expedition of Hernando de Soto, by the Gentleman of Elvas," Spanish

interior recovered a Spaniard by the name of Juan Ortíz

who had come to Florida with the Narváez expedition and

had been captured by the Indians. As a result of twelve

years in captivity Ortíz had developed proficiency as a

linguist, and served de Soto ably as an interpreter. The

expedition moved north from Ucita toward Apalachee pro-

vince and found the skeletons of horses that Narváez' men

had killed.[43] Moving through the Georgia country, de Soto

crossed the Savannah River to visit the important town of

Cufitachiqui[44] which was ruled by a female cacica who pro-

vided the soldiers with food. Showing little gratitude

for the hospitality, the Spaniards extracted a large

quantity of pearls from grave sites in the village. De

Soto took the cacica with him for some distance when he

---

Explorers, p. 146. Lewis locates Ucita near Charlotte
Harbor.

[43]Ibid., p. 171. Interestingly enough de Soto
carried hogs with him to Florida. Before he left the
Georgia country the herd had increased to almost three
hundred.

[44]Mary Ross locates Cufitachiqui near present-day
Columbia, South Carolina. See Mary Ross, "With Pardo and
Boyano on the Fringes of the Georgia Land," G.H.Q., XIV
(December, 1930), 273.

departed from Cufitachiqui. The expedition passed through South Carolina, North Carolina, Tennessee, back through Georgia and into Alabama. In the Alabama country the Spaniards visited the Indian village Coca,[45] where they remained almost a month. Leaving Coca, de Soto moved southward until he arrived at Mauvilla located possibly in Clarke County, Alabama.[46] De Soto burned the Mauvilla village and traveled into Mississippi. Misfortune set in and exacted a heavy toll. De Soto died May 21, 1541, and his men buried him in the Mississippi River to prevent the Indians from molesting his body. Luis Moscoso de Alvarado replaced de Soto as commander, and succeeded in building vessels substantial enough to get the remnants of the

---

[45] The United States de Soto Expedition Commission suggested that Coca or Coosa was near present-day Childersburg, Alabama. Recent archaeological investigations indicate otherwise. See David L. DeJarnette and Asael T. Hansen, The Archaeology of the Childersburg Site in Charles H. Fairbanks (ed.), Notes in Anthropology (Tallahassee: The Florida State University Press, 1960), pp. 61-62.

[46] Lewis suggests that Mauville "may have been located on the prairie north of the Black Warrior and east of the Tombigbee River in Green County, Alabama." See Lewis (ed.), "The Narrative of the Expedition of Hernando de Soto, by the Gentleman of Elvas," Spanish Explorers, p. 189.

expedition back to New Spain.[47]

Fray Luis Cáncer de Barbastro, a member of the Dominican Order, had his religious zeal stirred by talking to survivors of the de Soto expedition. Fray Gregorio de Beteta, a fellow Dominican, endorsed Fray Luis' idea of going to Florida. As a result, Fray Luis journeyed to Spain to plead his case and received permission to go to Florida. The priest departed from Vera Cruz for Florida in 1549 accompanied by several friars. The purpose of his expedition was to convert the Indians to Christianity rather than to explore or make known the interior. At the Bay of the Holy Spirit,[48] two of the religious party went ashore and met death at the hands of the Indians. Although his fellow compatriots counseled him against going, Fray Luis decided to go ashore. The Indians met the gallant friar at the water's edge and murdered him in full view of the expedition. The other members of the expedition, having witnessed this terrible act, determined

---

[47] Ibid., pp. 250-266.

[48] The Bay of the Holy Spirit was at Tampa. It received its name from Hernando de Soto. See Gannon, The Cross in the Sand, pp. 6-11.

not to go ashore, and the religious effort, so enthusi-
astically begun, came to naught.[49]

Ten years passed before Spanish forces visited
Florida again. During the interim the Spanish crown became increasingly anxious about the security of the peninsula, especially the Bahama Channel area. The treasure
fleet sailed through this sea lane on its return voyage
to Spain, and Spanish authorities did not wish control of
it to fall into the hands of another power. King Philip
II worried about the lack of a Spanish port of call to
assist vessels disabled by the frequent storms which occurred in the area. With these ideas in mind, the King
ordered Viceroy Luis de Velasco in New Spain to organize
an expedition to go to Florida to establish a colony. The
Viceroy chose Tristán de Luna y Arellano to command the
force which he gathered. Luna appeared to be well-
qualified to serve as the commander, for he had served
as second in command on the Coronado expedition. In
June, 1559, Don Tristán, with a large fleet and fifteen

---

[49]Kerrigan (trans.), Barcia's Chronological
History, pp. 26-27.

hundred individuals, set forth to colonize Florida. The

expedition landed either at Pensacola Bay or Mobile,[50] and

an unusually severe hurricane struck the would-be colo-

nists. The storm destroyed almost all of the ships and

most of the supplies. Luna's colony was in a difficult

position at the very beginning. Leaving a small force at

the landing site, the adelantado led most of the colonists

into Alabama in a search for food. The colonists spent a

lengthy period of time at Santa Cruz de Nanipacna.[51] Luna

dispatched a group from there to Coosa in a futile effort

to acquire food. Conditions did not improve, so the

settlers returned to Pensacola. Dissension broke out in

the ranks, and Angél de Villafañe relieved Luna of his

---

[50]The landing place of Tristán de Luna has precipitated a debate among historians which has not been resolved. Woodbury Lowery suggested Pensacola as the probable site. Lowery selected Pensacola as the basis of the
documentary evidence rather than on a personal inspection
of the area. Herbert Ingram Priestly, who wrote an excellent biography of Luna, accepted Lowery's conclusions.
The geographical features reported in the Luna account,
however, resemble the Mobile area more closely than
Pensacola.

[51]Herbert E. Bolton suggests Monroe County, Ala-
bama, as the probable location of Santa Cruz de Nanipacna.
See Herbert Eugene Bolton, The Spanish Borderlands (New
Haven: Yale University Press, 1921), pp. 131-132.

command. The new commander attempted to affect a settlement on the South Carolina coastline, but he failed to
find a site which he deemed suitable for a settlement.[52]

The failure of Tristán de Luna and Angél de Villafañe to establish a colony in Florida disappointed the
Spanish crown. The crown and the Council of the Indies
wondered whether this remote and desolate area merited
another colonization attempt at that time, for much money
and effort had been expended there already. Spanish authorities did not have to wait long for an answer to the
colonization debate. The Huguenots, anxious to create a
haven for themselves where they might avoid religious
persecution, sent an expedition to Florida in 1562 under
the command of Jean Ribaut. Ribaut established a small
colony near Paris Island, South Carolina,[53] and returned
to France to acquire additional supplies. The colony
failed utterly during his absence. Undaunted by this
failure the Huguenots tried again, this time further

---

[52] Herbert Ingram Priestly, *Tristán de Luna: Conquistador of the Old South* (Glendale: 1936), pp. 102-185.

[53] Jeannette Thurber Conner (trans.), *Jean Ribaut
the Whole and True Discovery of Terra Florida* (DeLand:
The Florida State Historical Society, 1927), pp. 58-97.

south. René de Laudonniérè (1564) commanded this expedition which established Fort Caroline at the mouth of the St. Johns River. Laudonniérè, however, was no leader of men. News of difficulty reached Admiral Coligny, and he dispatched Jean Ribaut with reinforcements and orders to take command of the fort.[54] The presence of the French interlopers did not go undetected. As such, they represented a serious threat to Spain's control of the Bahama Channel and the crown ordered the intruders evicted.

King Philip II of Spain turned to a most resolute and determined servant to remove the French menace from Florida. He selected Pedro Menéndez de Avilés, from the province of Asturias, for this important task. Menéndez had distinguished himself as a seaman in the service of the crown. He had served as Captain-General of the Fleet of the Indies and was a Knight in the Order of Santiago. Menéndez desired to go to Florida, for his only son, Juan, had been shipwrecked there and this was an opportunity to search for him. Also, Menéndez felt an obligation to

---

[54] Bolton, The Spanish Borderlands, pp. 136-137.

serve his king and God in removing the Huguenot usurp-

ers.[55] The adelantado assumed financial responsibility

for the expedition. The contract, dated March 20, 1565,

provided Menéndez with precise instructions. Pedro

Menéndez received orders to search thoroughly the Florida

coast to find the best harbor and place to establish a

colony and to expel any Europeans found who were not sub-

jects of the King of Spain. Missionaries accompanied the

expedition to convert the Indians to Christianity and to

provide religious services for the settlers. The crown

gave to Menéndez a grant of land twenty-five leagues

square and two fisheries, one for pearls and the other

for fish.[56]

Menéndez sailed from Spain with 2,646 persons con-

tained in thirty-four ships.[57] The adelantado appeared

---

[55] Jeannette Thurber Conner (trans.), Pedro Menéndez de Avilés Adelantado Governor and Captain-General of Florida, Memorial by Gonzalo Solis de Meras. First published in La Florida Su Conquista y Colonizacion por Pedro Menéndez de Avilés by Eugenio Ruidiaz y Caravia (Gainesville: University of Florida Press, Reprint, 1964), pp. 68-69.

[56] Ibid., pp. 259-270.

[57] Ibid., p. 74.

off Cape Cañaveral, August 28, 1565. Moving up the coast

Menéndez found a French fleet at anchor in the St. John

River. He engaged the French in an indecisive battle, and

then sailed down the coast where he began the establish-

ment of St. Augustine in September, 1565. Jean Ribaut set

out with a squadron of ships to attack Menéndez but was

blown by strong winds past St. Augustine. During his ab-

sence, Menéndez traveled overland to capture Fort Caroline

and to execute all the French who were not Catholics. The

Spaniards captured Ribaut when he tried to return overland

to Fort Caroline. They executed him and all of his fol-

lowers except Catholics. This decisive action by Menéndez

removed the French threat from Florida and established

Spanish supremacy in the area.[58]

---

[58]Ibid., pp. 80-122. Menéndez' act toward the
French has perpetrated a lively contest between historians, the heat of which can be felt to the present day.
To those of the "Leyenda Negra" school, such as Francis
Parkman, he represents the archtype of Spanish cruelty,
bigotry, and intolerance. Yet, Menéndez might be viewed
as a product of his age when such acts were perpetrated
by soldiers of other nations as well. All too frequently
the adelantado's splendid service to Spain has been over-
shadowed by his execution of the French. Menéndez awaits
still a definitive biographer. It will be difficult to
rehabilitate his image while this cloud of heat surrounds
him.

CHAPTER II

THE COLONIZATION OF FLORIDA AND SPANISH-

INDIAN RELATIONS, 1565-1656

In the removal of the French intruders, Pedro

Menéndez de Avilés had accomplished only one phase of his

mission in Florida.  He then set about to fortify the

area by establishing presidios and garrisons.  The ade-

lantado faced the problem also of exploring the interior

and extending the Christian faith to the Indians.  He laid

plans to induce farmers, artisans, and craftsmen to popu-

late and develop the region under his control.  The task

which he faced loomed colossal, but Menéndez took immedi-

ate steps to accomplish it.  Journeying southward from

St. Augustine, the governor established a garrison at the

Indian village of Ais, in the vicinity of Cape Cañaveral.

He christened this settlement Santa Lucía, rounded the

peninsula, and sailed up the western coast.  Stopping at

Charlotte Harbor,[1] he visited with Carlos, cacique of the Calusa Indians.[2] Pedro Menéndez impressed Cacique Carlos with his diplomacy, and Carlos presented his sister, Doña Antonia, to the governor as a bride. Menéndez accepted Doña Antonia to prevent ill-will among the Indians, but he carried her to Havana and placed her in a convent. The fact that Menéndez already had a wife and was a devout Catholic left him no other choice.[3]

In the spring of 1566, the governor advanced up the eastern coast of Florida, and stopped in Guale province where he visited with Chief Guale, principal chief of the area. The forces under this chieftain were at war with the natives of Orista province[4] who lived along the Carolina coast, and who were commanded by Cacique Orista.

---

[1] Charlotte Harbor is near present-day Tampa, Florida. See Swanton, Early History of the Creek Indians, p. 353.

[2] Chief Carlos was the cacique of the Calusa Indians. Connor (trans.), Pedro Menéndez de Avilés, p. 140.

[3] Connor (trans.), Pedro Menéndez de Avilés, pp. 147-152.

[4] The Orista tribe lived in the area of Port Royal and Charleston, South Carolina. See Swanton, Early History of the Creek Indians, p. 51.

Menéndez desired very much to put an end to this conflict, for he needed both groups of Indians as allies. Accordingly, he sought to affect a peace between the Guale and Orista Indians. Cacique Guale appeared willing to settle the dispute, so Menéndez departed to learn the sentiments of Chief Orista. The Florida governor found Cacique Orista equally disposed to put an end to the war with the Guale. Pedro Menéndez, pleased with the apparent success of his personal diplomacy, set about to select a good site for a fortress which he intended to serve as the nucleus of a settlement at Santa Elena.[5] The Spaniards named the presidio San Felipe, and Menéndez selected Esteban de las Alas to serve as the garrison commander. The adelantado, having completed this task, returned to Guale where he informed Cacique Guale of Cacique Orista's desire to conclude a peace.[6] Soon afterwards, peaceful relations prevailed between the Oristas and the Guale.

Three fortresses stood now along Florida's east

---

[5] Santa Elena was the Spanish equivalent for Port Royal, South Carolina.

[6] Connor (trans.), Pedro Menéndez de Avilés, pp. 138-179.

coast, and Menéndez turned his attention toward the interior of the southeast. The Florida governor commissioned Captain Juan Pardo to head an expedition consisting of more than a hundred men to explore into the interior. Captain Pardo received orders to befriend the Indians, to convert them to Christianity, and to travel as far as he could toward New Spain.[7] Menéndez hoped that an interior route could be established connecting Santa Elena with Zacatecas, Mexico. Such a road would obviate the necessity of shipping bullion around the Florida peninsula thereby protecting the rich cargo from exposure to pirate attack and inclement weather. Pardo led his party into the interior with these factors in mind. In present-day Polk County, North Carolina, Captain Pardo constructed a fortress, San Juan Xualla, and appointed Sergeant Hernando Boyano as the commander of the thirty man garrison.[8] Moving forward to Guatari, Pardo deposited a

---

[7] Mary Ross, "With Pardo and Boyano on the Fringes of the Georgia Land," G.H.Q., XIV (December, 1930), 269-270.

[8] Ibid., p. 275.

padre and four soldiers.[9]

Here, Pardo received orders from Menéndez to return
to Santa Elena to assume temporary command of the San
Felipe garrison. This prevented him from returning to
the interior until the fall of 1567.[10] Sergeant Boyano
traveled during Pardo's absence into western Georgia to
Chiaha located near present-day Rome, where he constructed
Fort Santa Elena.[11] He waited at Chiaha for Captain Pardo
to return to the expedition. Pardo, after rejoining
Boyano, traveled into the Alabama country in an effort to
reach the Indian village, Coca. Native hostility thwarted
his plans and forced him to turn back into the Georgia
country.[12] On his return trip to the Carolinas, Pardo
established a presidio at Cauchi.[13] He built a fort at

---

[9]Ibid., p. 277.

[10]J. G. Johnson, "The Spaniards in Northern Georgia
during the Sixteenth Century," G.H.Q., IX (June, 1925),
159.

[11]Ibid., p. 160.

[12]Ibid., p. 162.

[13]Ross, "With Pardo and Boyano on the Fringes of
the Georgia Land," G.H.Q., XIV (December, 1930), 282;
Johnson, "The Spaniards in Northern Georgia during the

Guatari and staffed it with a corporal and seventeen
soldiers,[14] and stationed thirty additional soldiers at
San Juan de Xualla.[15] Captain Pardo's expedition constituted a significant exploration of the interior southeast. Although not as long in distance as de Soto's
journey, the expedition members succeeded in fortifying
strategic parts of the interior area. These presidios
were the rudimentary beginnings of an interior defensive
system. Unfortunately, they received inadequate supplies
and had to be withdrawn soon afterwards.

Pedro Menéndez, while engaged in establishing defensive bastions to defend Florida, did not forget his
religious commitment to the Indian inhabitants. Fathers
belonging to the Society of Jesus arrived at St. Augustine
in 1566 to inaugurate missionary labors among the Indians.
Father Domingo Agustín, who went to work among the Guale

---

Sixteenth Century," G.H.Q., IX (June, 1925), 161. Ross
locates Cauchi in western North Carolina. Johnson feels
that Cauchi was in Georgia near the junction of the Santee
and Chattahoochee Rivers.

[14]Ross, "With Pardo and Boyano on the Fringes of
the Georgia Land," G.H.Q., XIV (December, 1930), 282.

[15]Ibid.

Indians, crowned his proselyting efforts by preparing a
grammar and a catechism for his neophytes written in their
native tongue.[16] All along the Florida littoral the Sons
of St. Ignatius endeavored in a vain attempt to establish
little spheres of religious influence. Success did not
reward their efforts. Several of the fathers suffered
death at the hands of the Indians they came to help.
Father Bautista de Segura, determined to establish a successful mission, decided to lead a group of Jesuits to
the Chesapeake Bay in 1570. This attempt met with misfortune as the Indians attacked and destroyed the mission.
Death, disease, and inadequate supplies exerted significant influence on the decision of the Jesuits to abandon
the Florida mission area in 1572.[17]

The Franciscans moved into Florida in 1573 to replace the Jesuits and to begin a long period of mission
work. Brown-robed friars fanned out over a good deal of

---

[16]Herbert Eugene Bolton and Mary Ross, The Debatable Land (Berkeley: University of California Press,
1925), p. 10.

[17]Gannon, The Cross in the Sand, pp. 32-34; Clif-
ford M. Lewis and Albert J. Loomie, The Spanish Jesuit
Mission in Virginia 1570-1577 (Chapel Hill: University of
North Carolina Press, 1953), pp. 28-45.

the southeast and their efforts met with success from the
start.  The mission system which they inaugurated extended
up the Georgia coast to Santa Elena, into Timucua, and
over into Apalachee.  The Franciscans did not totally neg-
lect the interior of the Georgia country and southern
Florida, but they concentrated their efforts in Guale,
Apalachee, and Timucua where the largest Indian popula-
tions lived.  The Franciscans had hardly arrived and established themselves on the mission field when the Indians
revolted against Spanish authority in Orista and Guale.
The San Felipe garrison, at Santa Elena, had faced a food
shortage in 1576, and to relieve pressure on the presidio
supplies, the commandant, Solis, decided to station a detachment of soldiers at the Oristan village, Escamacu.[18]

Lieutenant Hernando Boyano, who accompanied Pardo
into the interior in 1576, commanded the group of soldiers
sent to Escamacu.  The soldiers did not act with decorum
upon entering the village.  Their very presence, with

---

[18]Mary Ross, "French Intrusions and Indian Uprisings in Georgia and South Carolina," G.H.Q., VII (September, 1923), 253-254.  See also Ray E. Held, "Hernando de
Miranda, Governor of Florida 1575-1577," Florida Historical Quarterly, XXVIII (October, 1949), 125, hereinafter
cited as F.H.Q.

arquebuses and lighted tapers, frightened the villagers and most of them fled to the woods. The fact that the soldiers started immediately to take food from the Indians supply without any pretense of asking permission antago- nized the Orista. The village cacique did not run for cover in the woods. On the contrary, he remained out- wardly calm, and he joined into conversation with Boyano. Boyano permitted the cacique to influence him into order- ing the soldiers to extinguish their tapers. When they did this, the cacique summoned his braves who massacred Boyano and all of his followers except one named Calderón, who escaped to Santa Elena to warn of the uprising. The soldier's warning came none too soon, for the Indians laid siege to Santa Elena. A squadron from St. Augustine which carried the San Felipe garrison's pay stopped at Espogue in Guale, and the natives killed the entire company. Meanwhile, Governor Gutierre de Miranda arrived with a supply vessel at San Felipe while the siege was underway. Realizing the futility of maintaining the presidio in the face of this opposition, he dismantled the fortress and took the inhabitants back to St. Augustine.[19]

When Philip II learned about the Indian uprising, he sent Pedro Menéndez de Marqúez, nephew of the founder of St. Augustine, to Florida to replace Governor Miranda. Menéndez de Marqúez brought with him explicit orders to rebuild the presidio at Santa Elena. He restored the fort in the summer of 1577, and renamed the structure San Marcos.[20] The construction of the fortress was timely for a group of French intruders led by Nicolas Estrozi and Gilberto Gil made their appearance on the Florida coast and caused Governor Marqúez many anxious moments before he took effective action against them. Prior to the completion of San Marcos, Indian informants told Marqúez of a French fort situated to the north of Santa Elena. Alarmed by this information, the governor

---

[19] Ross, "French Intrusions and Indian Uprisings in Georgia and South Carolina," G.H.Q., VII (September, 1923), 254-256; Held, "Hernando de Miranda, Governor of Florida 1575-1577," F.H.Q., XXVIII (October, 1949), 125-126.

[20] Ross, "French Intrusions and Indian Uprisings in Georgia and South Carolina," G.H.Q., VII (September, 1923), 256. See also Mary Ross, "The Spanish Settlement of Santa Elena (Port Royal) in 1578," G.H.Q., VII (December, 1925), 353-355.

dispatched envoys to Spain to procure aid, and anxious
about the safety of St. Augustine he made a quick trip to
the Florida capital. This French intrusion only com-
pounded the anxiety caused by the rebellious Guale and
Orista Indians. Governor Marqúez learned that the Guale
Indians had called a war council to persuade all of the
province pueblos to join in the uprising against the
Spaniards. The governor sent representatives to the
council with instructions to ask the non-aligned Guale
to declare war on the malcontents headed by the cacique
of Espogue and to ask the Guale to deliver over to Spanish
authority any Frenchmen they had in their custody.
Finally Governor Marqúez traveled to Guale in an effort
to obtain the French whom he believed were hiding in the
Guale villages. Marqúez did not have a sufficient number
of men to back up his request with power politics if
necessary, and he failed in obtaining the cooperation of
the Indians.[21]  Governor Marqúez failed to achieve any

---

[21]Ross, "French Intrusions and Indian Uprisings in
Georgia and South Carolina," G.H.Q., VII (September,
1923), 259-260.

tangible results in Guale, so he proceeded northward to Santa Elena.

Meanwhile, an unidentified ship appeared off the coast which caused the San Marcos garrison considerable alarm. The alien craft disappeared from view, but the governor remained at Santa Elena for several days in the event that it reappeared. The ship did not return, so the governor hastened to St. Augustine to inquire whether the vessel had appeared in that vicinity. Menéndez arrived at the Florida capital and shortly afterwards two strange ships appeared off the entrance to the harbor, but they soon withdrew when the presidio guns fired at them. Marquéz concluded that the ships were of French origin, and that they were there in an attempt to rendezvous with their countrymen still among the Indians. The governor, wishing to prevent a rendezvous, decided to search for the fortress the intruders had constructed to the north of Santa Elena. He informed the fathers along the coast and the commandant at Santa Elena to inform him at once if they spotted any foreign vessels. Marquéz found the French fort north of Santa Elena, and destroyed it, but he succeeded in capturing no Frenchmen. To complicate

matters, the Guale and Orista Indians remained rebellious.[22]

Governor Marquéz made one final attempt to establish cordial relations with the cacique of Cayagua who
lived near Charleston, South Carolina. His efforts failed
as the Indians rebuffed his efforts with armed resistance.
The time had come to adopt a hard-fisted policy and
Marquéz did just that. He moved swiftly against the village Cocapoy, and the Indians delivered to him the French
they had in their possession. The governor then headed
toward Guale to deal with the malcontents there. Apparently the Guale Indians heard of Marquéz' new attitude,
for they swore allegiance to Spain and delivered the
French they had, including the leader of the intruders,
Nicolas Estrozi. Marquéz gave the captives a hasty trial,
and executed all but five of them.[23] The governor failed
to capture all of the intruders for some had gone far into
the interior, but he felt that the French in the interior
posed no real threat to St. Augustine. Just when it

---

[22]Ibid., pp. 260-266.

[23]Ibid., pp. 270-274.

appeared that the French threat had been ended, the governor received word of another intrusion. This time Marquéz
found the French in close proximity to St. Augustine, at
San Mateo. He defeated the French vessel in a pitched
battle and the captain, Gil, died in the skirmish.[24]
Later in the same year (1580) Spanish soldiers and priests
reported the appearance of more than twenty French vessels
off the Florida coast. The Guale Indians became restless
again, perhaps the result of additional French intrigue.
Marquéz put down their rebellion before it became serious.[25] Florida had a short breathing spell before the
next intruders arrived to threaten Spanish suzerainty in
the southeast.

England sponsored the next entry into Florida. Sir
Walter Raleigh, who was a court favorite of Queen Eliza-
beth, sent three expeditions to the southeast in an
abortive effort to establish a colony. Philip Amadas
and Arthur Barlowe led the first expedition which made a
landfall on Roanoke Island in 1584. They returned to

---

[24]Ibid., pp. 276-281.

[25]Ibid.

England and informed Raleigh of the undesirability of the site for a settlement, and recommended that an area in the Chesapeake Bay region be chosen. Richard Grenville and Ralph Lane commanded the second expedition. Ignoring Raleigh's orders the expedition landed at Roanoke in 1585. Grenville returned to England and left Lane in command of the colony. The colonists became disgruntled because of harsh living conditions, and they prevailed on Francis Drake, who stopped at the settlement in 1586, to carry them back to England. John White led the last of the Raleigh expeditions in 1587. He also went to Roanoke instead of looking for a more favorable location. White returned to England for a short visit, but naval warfare with Spain delayed his return to the colony. Some time during the interlude, the settlement vanished.[26]

Meanwhile Spain learned of Raleigh's expeditions and sent out reconnaissance missions in search of the intruders. Governor Pedro Menéndez de Marquéz searched

---

[26]Julian S. Corbitt (ed.), Papers Relating to the Navy During the Spanish War 1585-1587, XI (London: 1898), 24-27. See also J. Leitch Wright, Jr., "Sixteenth Century English-Spanish Rivalry in La Florida," F.H.Q., XXXVIII (April, 1960), 274-276.

the coast from St. Augustine to the Chesapeake Bay in 1587, but found no evidence of the English. The following year Vicente González sailed over the same area and, on his return trip to St. Augustine, he found the remains of the Raleigh colony.[27] The Indian revolts, the intrigue of the French, and Raleigh's attempt to establish a colony disturbed the Spaniards and caused anxious days in the eastern sector of the borderlands. Spain obtained a respite after the González reconnaissance of 1588. No serious disturbance occurred in Florida until the Yamassee Revolt of 1597.

During this interlude the business of securing the sea lanes and of converting the Indians went forward. Progress was not as significant as the Franciscans desired, as insufficient supplies and an inadequate number of friars retarded the religious effort. Indian uprisings and foreign intrusions had undermined spiritual gains. After 1593 Franciscan prospects appeared brighter and a substantial number of brothers who were sent immediately

---

[27] Wright, "Sixteenth Century English-Spanish Rivalry in La Florida," F.H.Q., XXXVIII (April, 1960), 274-276.

to the Guale missions, arrived to swell the ranks. There
they labored effectively until 1597 when a political
question arose which threatened to undo all the religious
gains. Father Corpa, stationed at Tolomato,[28] rebuked
Juanillo, heir to the cacique of Guale for being a biga-
mist. Juanillo continued his polygamy, however, and
Father Corpa informed him that he had forfeited his succession rights to the caciqueship. Angered by what he
considered to be high-handed treatment, Juanillo set about
to organize a rebellion designed to wreck the Franciscan
missionary program. Juanillo and the malcontents moved
from mission to mission killing the priests and burning
the churches. Almost overnight years of Franciscan efforts were undone. A full-scale Indian rebellion arose
in Guale reminiscent of the 1577-1580 disturbances.
Governor Gonzalo Mendez de Canzo employed stern measures
in his move against the Guale insurgents. The soldiers
burned the Indian crops inflicting severe food shortages.
The loyalty of Dona Aña, cacica of San Pedro on Cumberland

---

[28] Tolomato was located close to the mouth of the
Altamaha River. See John T. Lanning, The Spanish Missions
of Georgia (Chapel Hill: University of North Carolina
Press, 1935), p. 3.

Island stopped the advance of the rebellious Indians toward St. Augustine. Although much of Guale lay in ruins, the rebellion had been contained.[29]

January, 1600, Governor Canzo received royal instructions to release any rebellious captives that he had in his possession. He dispatched Sergeant-Major Alonzo Díaz de Badajoz northward to begin an investigation of Guale province to ascertain whether any rebellious tendencies still existed. Apparently the rebellion had lost all of its attractiveness for Chief Espogache affirmed his loyalty to the crown and indicated a desire for peace. Another example of Indian penitence occurred in May, 1600, when a delegation came to St. Augustine and expressed its desire to regain Spanish good will. Soon afterwards, Governor Canzo set out to investigate Guale personally. He learned the fate of the Tolomato rebels at Talaxe, near the mouth of the Altamaha River. They told him that they had killed Don Francisco, the cacique, and his heir,

---

[29]J. G. Johnson, "The Yamassee Revolt of 1597 and the Destruction of the Georgia Missions," G.H.Q., VII (March, 1923), 44-53; Lanning, The Spanish Missions of Georgia, pp. 82-109; Gannon, The Cross in the Sand, pp. 40-42.

Juanillo, who instigated the rebellion. The Talaxeans
expressed their desire to become obedient vassals once
again, and Father Pedro Ruíz absolved them. As Governor
Canzo moved up the coast cacique after cacique reaffirmed
his loyalty to Spain. In the middle of February, 1602,
six caciques conferred with the governor at St. Catherines
and proclaimed their subservience. Father Ruíz absolved
them of their sins and Guale province was obedient
again.[30] The time appeared opportune to return the
Franciscan friars to the mission fields, and Governor
Canzo sent them back to Guale.

The Crown learned of the Guale uprising and its
unfortunate results. Some members of the Council of the
Indies suggested that an investigation of Florida was in
order. They pointed out that the Crown had invested a
good deal of money in the defensive and missionary programs there. In addition, the Councillors noted that St.
Augustine was not the best port in Florida because of its
shallow bar. The poor soil, in the environs of the

---

[30] Mary Ross, "The Restoration of the Spanish Missions in Georgia, 1598-1606," G.H.Q., X (September, 1926),
173-180.

capital city, failed to produce sufficient food to support
the inhabitants. As a result, Florida imported most of
its provisions in the form of a subsidy from New Spain.
Three possible courses of action presented themselves: to
reduce the importance of St. Augustine as the primary base
and concentrate on Santa Elena or a deep-water site in
Guale, to abandon the capital city, or, as a final resort,
to remove Spain's defensive and mission system from
Florida and concentrate efforts in Cuba. Governor Canzo
was unaware of these developments when he returned to St.
Augustine pleased with the results of his visit.[31] Meanwhile, the Crown had decided to investigate conditions in
Florida.

King Philip III sent orders to Governor Pedro
Valdés of Cuba to go to Florida and conduct an investi-
gation. Governor Valdés did not want to leave the com-
fort of Havana to visit the crude outpost of St.
Augustine, so he sent Fernando, his son, in his place.
Don Fernando Valdés conducted his inquiry at St. Augustine

---

[31] Charles W. Arnade, Florida on Trial 1593-1602
(Coral Gables: University of Miami Press, 1959), pp.
1-90.

in the fall of 1602. The Governor's son heard the testimony of eighteen witnesses and all but Gutierrez Ecija stressed the importance of maintaining the presidio at St. Augustine. They asserted that a foreign power would occupy the place if Spain abandoned it. The witnesses agreed with unanimity that Florida was no "otro Mexico," and their testimony revealed that the lack of food was probably the most urgent problem. Franciscan fathers thought that problems with the Indians resulted from the inadequate support that Canzo gave to the missionary effort. They desired to relocate Florida's capital nearer to Guale, where better harbor sites existed, and where most of the missionaries worked at the time. Canzo, himself, held out in his determination to keep the capital at St. Augustine, and above all he did not wish to see Florida abandoned. He told of his efforts to stimulate agriculture, and remarked that he wanted to develop Tama, a vague region west of Guale in interior Georgia as a possible solution to the food problem. Governor Valdés forwarded the information to the Council of the Indies which considered the fate of Florida. The Council decided against the relocation of St. Augustine or the drastic alternative of abandoning Florida. It chose, instead, to send Pedro de Ybarra to replace Canzo as governor.[32]

French interlopers appeared again in Florida in 1605. They came to trade for sassafras, ginsing, and deerskins, all of which existed in significant quantities in Guale, Orista, and Cayagua. An alien vessel first appeared off the entrance to the harbor of St. Augustine in February, 1605. Soon afterwards it reached Cumberland Island, where the resident friar dispatched a mission Indian to learn the identity of the craft. He reported that it was a French vessel, and then the padre sent a messenger to inform the St. Augustine authorities. Indians on St. Catherine's Island also forwarded a warning to the Florida capital of the ship's appearance and attacked a French crew which rowed ashore. Governor Ybarra learned from the St. Catherine report that the vessel was large, and dispatched Francisco de Ecija in a ship to engage the enemy.[33]

The frigate, San José, arrived at St. Augustine

---

[32]Ibid.

[33]Mary Ross, "The French on the Savannah 1605," G.H.Q., VIII (September, 1924), 184-192.

shortly afterwards, and Ybarra sent it northward under the
command of the Alférez Martín de Boyano to assist Ecija.
The arrival of still another Spanish frigate proved opportune, and Governor Ybarra dispatched this vessel also to
Guale. Ecija and his assistants spotted the alien craft
anchored in the Savannah River and the Spanish vessels
blocked the exit to the sea. A hot battle ensued but the
outnumbered French were no match for the Spanish sailors
and Ecija towed the enemy bark and its prisoners in tri-
umph to St. Augustine. Ecija scouted the area as far as
Cape Fear, and the reconnaissance revealed the presence of
no additional vessels.[34] The role which the Guale Indians
played pleased Governor Ybarra. Not only had the Indians
reported the presence of the French, but they attacked one
of the crews. This was a most encouraging development,
for only a few years earlier they had revolted and forced
the Franciscans from the mission fields.

The return of the Franciscans to the Guale missions
had proved fortunate for the Spanish government. The very
alertness of the friars and their neophytes had not

---

[34]Ibid., pp. 184-193.

permitted the presence of the French to go undetected.

Hardly had the fathers resumed their stations when Florida
received an episcopal visitation from the Bishop of Cuba,
Juan de la Cabezas de Altamirano. The Bishop visited the
missions of Guale and Timucua to confirm the neophytes.
Altogether Bishop Altamirano confirmed more than two
thousand Indians and Spaniards, and ordained several individuals into the ministry. In broadest outline the ecclesiastical visit showed that the efforts in Florida had
not been in vain. It pleased Bishop Altamirano that the
religious work progressed so smoothly, considering the
rebellions that had taken place in the mission field in
recent times.[35]

Soon after Bishop Altamirano inspected the state of
religious affairs in Florida, news reached Spain of an
English settlement on the Chesapeake Bay. The policy
which the Crown adopted in this instance was out of
character with the measures Spain had taken in the past
with respect to foreign intrusions into Florida. Spain

---

[35]Ross, "The Restoration of the Spanish Missions in
Georgia, 1598-1606," G.H.Q., X (September, 1926), 186-192.

sent no expeditions to expel the Jamestown settlers as she had to oust Laudonniérè, but merely dispatched reconnaissance missions to spy on the settlement. Fortunately for St. Augustine the garrison received no reduction in soldiers. In 1609 and again in 1611 expeditions departed from St. Augustine to reconnoiter the coast to gather as much information about the English settlement as possible. Governor Ybarra felt that the English should be driven out, for he knew that their next advance would be further south within easy striking distance of St. Augustine. In Spain a Council of War petitioned the King also to take positive measures to expel the English before their settlement had a chance to take root. Yet the King did not give the order. He hoped evidently that the Chesapeake colony would prove to be as expensive to the English as the Florida settlements had been to the Spanish, and their economic situation would cause the English authorities to abandon it. [36]

Spain had an excellent opportunity to expel the

[36] Irene A. Wright (trans.), "Spanish Policy Toward Virginia 1606-1612, Jamestown, Ecija, and John Clark of the Mayflower," American Historical Review, XXV (April, 1920), 448-479.

Jamestown settlers before 1612. The colony had a poor beginning as disease, climate, and inadequate supplies exerted a devastating effect. The site selected for the
settlement was poor. Too many men came to Jamestown preferring to search for gold rather than to work. It took
the rigid discipline of John Smith to point the colonists
in a more positive direction. A Spanish expedition could
have destroyed Jamestown had the orders come to attack
while the English struggled to exist, but no such orders
came. The enemy had established himself but the vigil of
the area between Jamestown and St. Augustine had to be
maintained. Although Spain claimed the coastal area as
far north as Labrador, her actual control extended no
further than Santa Elena, South Carolina.

Florida governors did not concentrate all of their
energies on the coastal presidios and Guale missions. In
the seventeenth century increased attention was focused
on the interior regions of Timucua and Apalachee. Father
Martín Prieto performed yeoman service in the Franciscan
advance into interior Florida by visiting the Timucuan
towns in 1607 and establishing contact with the Apalachee
villages in 1608. Not to be outdone was Father Francisco

Pareja who wrote a grammar, a dictionary, and religious tracts in the Timucuan language much as Father Agustín had done earlier for the Guale.[37] In spite of the fact that missionaries had labored in Timucua since 1565, Apalachee province was largely ignored until 1633 when a contingent of Franciscans traveled into the area.[38] An insufficient number of friars and inadequate supplies retarded the advance into western Florida. The Fathers found the Timucuan and Apalachee inhabitants receptive to religious instruction, and in 1639, Governor Damián Castro y Pardo wrote to the Crown requesting additional missionaries. He pointed proudly to the fact that more than a thousand Indians had accepted Christianity and he anticipated many more converts when the religious force received reinforcements.[39]

While the Franciscan missionaries moved further

---

[37]Gannon, The Cross in the Sand, pp. 51-54.

[38]Lanning, The Spanish Missions of Georgia, p. 166.

[39]Carta a S. M. de Damian de la Vega Castro y Pardo Sobre Varios Asuntos de la Florida, August 22, 1639, in Manuel Serrano y Sanz, Documentos Historicos de la Florida y la-Luisiana Siglos XVI al XVIII (Madrid: Biblioteca de los Americanistas, 1912), p. 198.

into the interior, news reached St. Augustine of an
English intrusion into the Georgia country. Immediately
Governor Juan de Salinas dispatched an expedition into
the interior of present-day Georgia and Carolina to investigate the rumor. The search made in 1624 was thorough
but the scouting party encountered no Englishmen. Four
years later, Pedro de Torres searched essentially over the
same area investigating rumors of English appearances in
the interior but he failed also to encounter any intruders.[40]

The expeditions sent in search of English intruders
did not hinder seriously Spanish expansion into Apalachee
province. Apalachee soon became noted for its food producing qualities. Spanish ships stopped frequently at
St. Marks to acquire cargoes of corn, beans, deerskins,
and wild turkeys.[41] Tranquility did not prevail always
in Apalachee. The mission neophytes rebelled as they had
on the Guale coast in the past. Apalachee mission Indians
revolted in 1647 and put to death three of the resident

---

[40]Bolton and Ross, The Debatable Land, pp. 24-25.

[41]Ibid., p. 26.

Franciscans. The Royal Treasurer, Francisco Menéndez Marqúes, put the uprising down quickly. He executed the principal leaders of the revolt and sentenced others to hard labor at the St. Augustine presidio.[42]

With the Apalachee rebellion put down, Governor Benito Ruíz de Salazar inaugurated an experiment in food production in the province which he felt might solve Florida's most pressing problem. Florida had not been able to produce sufficient food for its Spanish populace since colonization under Pedro Menéndez de Avilés. As a result the crown had to send a situado or subsidy to maintain the various garrisons. Red tape, official negligence, bad weather and a host of other factors frequently prevented the supply vessels from arriving on time. At times the subsidy was several years in arrears. When it did arrive, more often than not much of the food had spoiled. This subsidy did not solve Florida's inadequate food problem.[43] Governor Salazar knew that Apalachee

---

[42]Lanning, The Spanish Missions of Georgia, p. 168; Gannon, The Cross in the Sand, p. 56.

[43]Verne Elmo Chatelaine, The Defenses of Spanish Florida 1565-1763 (Washington: Carnegie Institution Publication 511, 1914), p. 9.

possessed fertile soil and his immediate design was to see
if wheat could be grown in the area around San Luis. He
ordered wheat seeds planted, and requested a miller be
sent to Florida from the Canary Islands. Salazar died before the miller arrived. Apparently his successors[44] had
no interest in the project. The planted crop spoiled in
the fields, and there was no effort to continue the experiment. The Apalachee Indians saved seeds from the ex-
perimental plot, and they produced enough grain in future
years to require no longer that the Spanish supply them
with flour.[45]

Although the agricultural experiment failed in
Apalachee, not all was bleak in Florida. Between 1647
and 1656 no Indian revolts or disturbances occurred.
During this tranquil period Franciscan missionaries
busied themselves with increasing efforts. The spector
of revolt did not haunt the mission fields or threaten

---

[44]His successors were Nicolas Ponce de Leon, Pedro
Benedit Horruytiner, and Diego de Rebolledo.

[45]Katherine S. Lawson, "Governor Salazar's Wheat
Farm Project 1647-1657," F.H.Q., XXXIV (January, 1956),
196-200.

to undo the labor of several years. Annually the number
of converts to Catholicism increased significantly. In
essence a sort of "Golden Age" of religious activity prevailed in Guale, Apalachee, and Timucua. When the year
1655 dawned, Franciscan authorities reported 26,000
Christian Indians located in thirty-eight religious doctrinas or districts. Also there were seventy Franciscans
in Florida engaged in religious activity. The mission
program had reached a high degree of development.[46]

---

[46]Gannon, The Cross in the Sand, p. 57.

CHAPTER III

GOVERNOR DIEGO DE REBOLLEDO'S VISITA GENERAL

OF APALACHEE AND TIMUCUA, JANUARY 17

TO FEBRUARY 13, 1657

Spain maintained a good relationship with the Indians from 1647 to 1655. The Catholic Church gained converts almost daily and the mission system flourished. The
Spanish army experienced a respite also, but the calm
broke dramatically in 1656. The Timucuan Indians rose up
in rebellion and the discontent spread to Apalachee.
Governor Diego de Rebolledo took immediate measures to
put down the rebellion and to punish the instigators. He
sent Sergeant-Major Adrian de Cañicares and sixty infantrymen to quell the disorder. Spaniards subdued the
Timucuans quickly and executed eleven of the Indians to
provide an example for future trouble-makers. The
Apalachees received no punishment since they did not
assume a major role in the rebellion. Governor Rebolledo

stationed a lieutenant and twelve soldiers at San Luis to guard against a future uprising.[1]

Governor Rebolledo (1651-1657), a member of the Military Order of Santiago, departed for the scene of the rebellion in November, 1656. His basic purpose was to conduct a visita or visitation of Timucua and Apalachee. The governor passed through Timucua and actually began his inspection in Apalachee in January of 1657. Don Joseph de Prado, the Royal Treasurer, Friar Antonio Esteban, Sergeant-Major Adrian de Cañicares, Sergeant-Major Salvador de Zigarro, Francisco de Ruedo, Juan Moreno y Segovia and a few soldiers from the St. Augustine garrison accompanied Governor Rebolledo and served as his assistants. Rebolledo promulgated an auto at the Indian village, San Damían de Cupaica, which set forth the purpose and objective of his trip to the area. The governor noted that he came to West Florida to insure that no vestiges of the rebellion remained. He pointed out that he intended to conduct a general inspection of the province as this had not been done in some time. The governor's auto ordered

---

[1]Swanton, Early History of the Creek Indians, p. 338.

all of the caciques and principal men of San Damían and
its environs to appear before him in the village council
house. Governor Rebolledo indicated that he intended to
discuss several items of importance with the assembled
Indians. Stability of the Indian towns loomed large on
the agenda. The governor decided since the rebellion had
just ended, to discuss with the tribal leaders the importance of maintaining an orderly and peaceful government. He considered this to be an essential ingredient
to insure the general welfare of the village. The governor expressed his intention, in the auto, to question the
Apalachees to ascertain if they had been mistreated by
anyone, to hear any complaints they had, and to see that
justice prevailed in every instance. The royal scribe,
Juan Moreno y Segovia posted the auto in a prominent place
in the village to expedite the visita proceedings.[2]

On January 17, in San Damían, there appeared before
Governor Rebolledo, Baltasar, cacique of San Damían;
Bentura, cacique of San Cosme; and Lucas, cacique of San
Lucas. Most of the principal men of the environs

---

[2]Ibid.

accompanied their respective caciques. Diego Salvador, the interpreter for Governor Rebolledo, read and explained the auto to the assembled group. Baltasar, the cacique of San Damián served as the spokesman for the group of caciques and principal men. The cacique declared to the governor that he carried out promptly the orders of the Spanish, and that the Indians of his jurisdiction willingly rendered assistance to the Franciscan friars who labored among them. But the cacique testified that the friars forced the Indians to carry heavy loads to St. Augustine frequently. As a result, the Indians hesitated to go to the Florida capital because of the burdens which the priests ordered them to carry. He admitted that the present padre, Bernardo de Santa María, did not require the Indians to serve as cargo bearers, and for this respite the Indians were grateful.[3]

The San Damián cacique's testimony revealed that his vassals had endured not only the rigors of the St. Augustine portage, but they had been required to go to

---

[3] Auto para hacer [la] Vicita General en la provincia de Apalache, January 16, 1657, Stet. Coll. Escrib. de Cam., Leg. 155, p. 1.

the provinces of the infidel Apalachocoli[4] and the Chaca-
tos[5] to bring back skins and other esteemed items. Some
of the Indians died on these journeys without the opportunity to confess because of the excessive burdens which
they carried. The cacique asked Governor Rebolledo in
view of past occurrences to relieve the Indians from com-
pulsory portage duty. Baltasar beseeched the governor to
allow the Indians to perform their ceremonial dances on
festive days and to play the ball game. Baltasar argued
that the Franciscans had reflected excessive zeal with
respect to tribal customs.[6]

---

[4]The exact location of the Apalachocoli or Apalachicola is uncertain, but apparently they lived along
the Chattachoochee River above its confluence with the
Flint. See Swanton, Early History of the Creek Indians,
pp. 125-134.

[5]The precise location of the Chacato or Chatot is
equally difficult to determine. Swanton placed them "west
of the Apalachicola River, somewhere near the middle
course of the Chipola." See Swanton, Early History of
the Creek Indians, p. 134.

[6]Vicita de San Damían de Cupaica, January 17,
1657, Stet. Coll. Escrib. de Cam., Leg. 155, pp. 2-3.
San Damían de Cupaica was located approximately 88
leagues west of St. Augustine. See Lucy L. Wenhold
(trans.), "A 17th Century Letter of Gabriel Díaz Vara
Calderón, Bishop of Cuba, Describing the Indians and

Governor Rebolledo inquired whether the soldiers of St. Augustine or any individuals outside of the district mistreated them in any way, if they confiscated personal possessions, or forced the Indians to provide food for them. The governor promised to correct any abuses which existed. Baltasar pointed out that when an Indian from outside his jurisdiction arrived in the area that his subjects conducted him to their homes and shared their food and shelter with him. Any soldiers who came received food and shelter also, for the Indians felt an obligation to them. Baltasar asserted that the Franciscans had attempted to prohibit these practices. Prior to the arrival of Friar Bernardo de Santa María in 1656, the padres prohibited the Indians from carrying cargo for the soldiers and other Spaniards who came to the village. The Fathers told the Indians that they had work enough for them to do, and threatened to punish them if they worked for the soldiers. When frigates arrived from Havana, the padres refused permission for the Indians to go down to

the wharf to help unload the vessels or to carry anything
to the dock. In this way, the padres prevented the Indians from selling items to the ship's crew and earning
money. On the other hand, the Fathers bought the Indian's merchandise for a very low price and made a good
profit when they sold them to the sailors who came to the
port. In addition, the Fathers forced the Indians to
carry the cargo to the wharf without paying them anything
for their efforts.[7]

Governor Rebolledo inquired of Cacique Baltasar if
any of the Indians in his area lived immoral lives, and
if any of the vassals refused to obey his orders. Also,
Governor Rebolledo wished to know whether there had been
any murders or if any Indian maintained a concubine.
Rebolledo felt that the possession of a concubine set a
bad example before the other males and violated Christian
precepts. Cacique Baltasar admitted that some of his subjects had maintained concubines before Lieutenant Antonio
de Sertucha came to the province. The lieutenant, learning of this condition, put an end to it. None existed to

---

[7]Vicita de San Damían de Cupaica, January 17, 1657,
Stet. Coll. Escrib. de Cam., Leg. 155, p. 4.

his knowledge at the time. Baltasar had no grievance to make about Sertucha's conduct of office, nor did other Indians present in the council house reflect discontent with the lieutenant's administration. In fact, the Indians indicated their esteem for him. The cacique had no complaint about the soldiers either, for they treated the Indians fairly and their conduct set a good example before his vassals.[8]

Governor Rebolledo turned to the other caciques and principal men present in the council house to learn if they had any complaints or statements to make. The Indians had no grievances or questions to present, and he told them that he intended to provide all of the Apalachee villages with regulations designed to insure stability in the villages. He warned the Indians that they had to observe these rules. The governor then turned his attention to the defensive structure of the area. Governor Rebolledo expressed, especially, his firm intention of keeping the English out of Apalachee. He admitted that the English made a successful raid at St. Marks the year before

---

[8] Ibid., pp. 4-5.

(1656), but that he did not intend for alien intrusions to occur again. Governor Rebolledo affirmed that he did not intend for the infidel Indians[9] who lived hearby to harass or bother the Apalachees. The governor explained to the Indians that he had placed a garrison of infantrymen in Apalachee not to inconvenience the Indians but to defend the province against enemy incursions. Baltasar and the other caciques expressed their pleasure with this move. Governor Rebolledo concluded his inspection of San Damían de Cupaica[10] and provided the assembled Indian leaders with a series of regulations.

The first regulation pertained to Indians who served as cargo bearers. It stipulated emphatically that no Indian was to carry cargoes to St. Augustine unless the governor sent an order granting permission for him to perform this service. Rebolledo included two exceptions in the order. The Indians were to carry the food and bed roll of a soldier dispatched by the governor and the

---

[9]The reference here is probably to the Apalachicolas and Chatot.

[10]Vicita de San Damían de Cupaica, January 17, 1657, Stet. Coll. Escrib. de Cam., Leg. 155, p. 5.

Indian had the privilege, if he chose, to carry such cargo
for others, provided that he received compensation for his
services. Governor Rebolledo permitted no other exception. If an Indian wished to provide a soldier with food
he could not be refused this gesture of friendship. Any
other services that he provided for a soldier had to be
paid for by the infantryman. Similarly, Governor Rebolledo decreed that no person could prohibit the Indians
from trading or doing business with any Spaniard. In the
event the Indians carried a cargo to the sea, with reference to the friars, they had to receive compensation for
their services. No Indian could go out from Apalachee to
trade with the heathen Indians such as the Chatot or
Apalachicolas without first obtaining permission from the
governor or from the lieutenant of the province.[11]

Governor Rebolledo permitted the Indians to perform
their ceremonial dances as long as they were not offensive
to the church. In addition, he granted the Apalachees
permission to play the ball game as long as the game did

_____

[11]Aranzes que se dio a todos los lugares de
Apalache, January 17, 1657, Stet. Coll. Escrib. de Cam.,
Leg. 155, pp. 6-7.

not injure them or interfere with their daily obligations.
Spain's recognition of social stratification among the
Indians is clearly evidenced in the fifth regulation.
Governor Rebolledo set down the rule that when a cacique
or principal man broke a civil or religious regulation no
one could mete out to that individual any type of punishment.  Before any action could be taken the governor had
to be informed of the nature of the offense.  Based on
this information the governor would determine the proper
course of action and then inform the provincial authorities of his decision.  Governor Rebolledo's final regulation related to commercial transactions.  He decreed with
respect to buying and selling products of the area, such
as food, that they would maintain the present method of
operation.[12]  This system of regulations was an attempt
by the governor to maintain tight control over the Indians
through a well-defined policy.

Governor Rebolledo conducted his next investigation
at the village Santa María de Bacuqua on the nineteenth of
January.  There appeared before him Alonso, the principal

---

[12]Ibid.

cacique of Santa María, and Martín, cacique of Guaca, a
town under the jurisdiction of Santa María, as well as the
principal men. Diego Salvador, who served as the governor's interpreter, read and explained the auto to the
group. Cacique Martín of Guaca served as the spokesman
for his colleagues. He informed Governor Rebolledo that
neither he nor his fellow caciques had any grievance to
declare with respect to the lieutenant and the garrison
that had been stationed in the province. To the contrary,
the Indians explained that the Spanish soldiers had shown
them and their people many kindnesses. The Indians also
expressed their gratitude to the governor, which they
never failed to do, for the fact that the soldiers had not
made any demands on them. The Indians, in return for this
kind treatment, gave food to the Spanish soldiers as a
voluntary act of friendship. Cacique Martín commented
that his people wished very much to have the military
force stationed in the province permanently. The soldiers, Martín declared, set excellent examples of conduct
for the Indians, and they defended them from the hostile

actions of the heathern Indians who lived nearby.[13] This

typical statement of such excellent relations with the

soldiers suggests that Rebolledo was trying to marshall

his evidence to make the report favor his administration.

Cacique Martín, moreover, made a grievance about a

Franciscan friar who served in the province at the pueblo

of San Pedro de Patali. The cacique and the principal men

had gone to San Pedro to await the arrival of the influ-

ential cacique of San Luis de Talimali whom they highly

respected. They decided upon the cacique's arrival to

celebrate a festival in his honor. They had hardly built

their fires and set out the dishes of food when Friar

Francisco Pascual appeared on the scene. Angered by the

festivities, the friar picked up a piece of wood and broke

all the containers of food. Friar Pascual's conduct em-

barrassed and puzzled the Indians, for the Father had

---

[13]Vicita del lugar [Santa María] de Bacuqua, January 19, 1657, Stet. Coll. Escrib. de Cam., Leg. 155, pp.
7-10. Santa María de Bacuqua was located approximately 86
leagues west of St. Augustine. Santa María de Bacuqua is
not in the mission list of 1675 by that precise name. San
Antonio de Bacuqua is listed. Probably the two pueblos
are the same. See Lucy L. Wenhold (trans.), "A 17th Century Letter of Gabriel Díaz Vara Calderón," p. 8.

shamed them in public without any indication that they had misbehaved. The bewildered and confused Indians fled into the forest for fear of further reprisal. The Indians asked Governor Rebolledo to prevent such a reoccurrence. Cacique Martín indicated to Rebolledo that this was not an isolated instance for the Franciscans had punished other caciques in the province and he beseeched Rebolledo to take the necessary measures to insure that this did not happen again.[14]

Equally important but more immediate was the short-age of food which Santa María faced. The village was an old one, and the fields had lost much of their fertility. As a result the Indians produced poor harvests. To com-pound the problem, the woods had been cleared to such an extent that the Indians experienced difficulty in obtain-ing fire wood. Because of this sad condition, the Indians asked Governor Rebolledo to permit them to relocate their village a half league from its present location where

---

[14]Vicita del lugar [Santa María] de Bacuqua, Janu-ary 19, 1657, Stet. Coll. Escrib. de Cam., Leg. 155, pp. 7-10.

there existed sufficient land to satisfy their demands.[15]

Cacique Martín made it clear that his criticism of
Friar Pascual's conduct in no way reflected a personal
antagonism toward the church.  Being a religious man, he
was aware that the Indians needed food not only for the
body but the spirit as well.  He emphasized the fact that
his village, unlike others in the province, possessed no
church or missionary.  Consequently there was no one to
teach the Indians Christian doctrine, to say mass, or to
hear confession.  The other pueblos had someone to minis-
ter to their spiritual needs, and the cacique asked Governor Rebolledo to provide his subjects with a priest.
Governor Rebolledo granted permission to Cacique Martín
to relocate Santa María de Bacuqua and promised to ask
the Reverend Padre Provincial at St. Augustine to send a
priest to the village.  The governor asked if there existed any strife in the pueblo, if any Indians had committed murders, or other "scandalous offenses," and if
the tribesmen disobeyed the mandates of the cacique.  The
Indians answered no to all these questions.  Governor

---

[15]Ibid.

Rebolledo then provided the cacique with a copy of the aranzes, and he concluded his investigation of the town the same day.[16]

The governor traveled from Santa María de Bacuqua to the nearby pueblo of San Pedro de Patali, where, on the same day, he conducted another inquiry. In the council house there appeared before the governor, Baltasar, cacique of San Pedro; Francisco, cacique of Ayamano; Alonso, cacique of Talapaliqui; and the principal men of the aforementioned villages. The interpreter, Diego Salvador read the auto de visita to the Indians, and Cacique Baltasar served as the principal spokesman for the Indians.[17] Baltasar testified that the soldiers of the Apalachee garrison had not mistreated his people, nor had any other emissaries of Governor Rebolledo who had come to the pueblo. As in the case of Cacique Martín, Baltasar swore that the military had treated his subjects

---

[16]Ibid.

[17]Vicita del lugar de San Pedro de Patali, January 19, 1657, Stet. Coll. Escrib. de Cam., Leg. 155, pp. 10-12. San Pedro de Patali was located approximately 84 leagues west of St. Augustine. See Lucy L. Wenhold (trans.), "A 17th Century Letter of Gabriel Díaz Vara Calderón," p. 8.

with kindness and like the people of Santa María de
Bacuqua, the Indians of San Pedro de Patali provided
voluntarily food and other necessities for the soldiers.
Relations with the padres did not fare as well. Baltasar
indicated that in some parts of Apalachee province the
Franciscans punished caciques and principal men as well
as their vassals. Apparently, the friars made no exception in the type of punishment meted out to vassal or
master, for they lashed both ignominiously with whips.
This action had caused a discipline problem, for the vassals had become disobedient as a result of their cacique's
humiliation. The situation, Baltasar warned, had to be
corrected if discipline and order were to prevail.[18]

Governor Rebolledo asked the Indians if the military forces of Apalachee forced the Indians to carry
cargoes for them. Baltasar affirmed that neither the
lieutenant or the soldiers had obligated the Indians to
serve as porters. Baltasar volunteered additional information about the Franciscans who in past years had forced

---

[18]Vicita del lugar de San Pedro de Patali, January
19, 1657, Stet. Coll. Escrib. de Cam., Leg. 155, pp. 10-
12.

his vassals to carry loads to the heathen Indian villages and to bring back doeskins and other items. He complained that this took a good deal of his vassals' time, forcing them to leave their families and their own domestic occupations. This disruption would have been tolerable, Baltasar explained in a critical tone, if the Indians had received payment for their services, but only Juan, a principal man of his village, had received recompense.[19]

Governor Rebolledo asked Baltasar as he did in Santa María and San Pedro whether any murders had occurred in the village or if feuds or public scandals existed. The governor also questioned Baltasar to learn if he commanded the proper respect of his subjects. The cacique indicated that he had no knowledge of any disorders and that his subjects payed him homage. Rebolledo, pleased with Baltasar's statements, ordered the interpreter, Salvador, to read to the assembly the series of rules that he had given to the other villages and ordered the Indians to abide by them. The governor then closed the

---

[19] Ibid.

investigation and dismissed the Indians.[20]

Governor Rebolledo arrived at San Juan de Aspalaga on January 20, 1657, but was unable to conduct a visita. He found neither the caciques nor their principal men present in the village. Rebolledo made an inquiry to ascertain the reason for their absence. He learned that the tribal leaders had gone to visit the Junumelas, an Indian group which lived nearby. Deciding to delay their visita to a later date, he went to San Luis and instructed one of the village Indians to go in search of the cacique and to inform him and his principal men to come to San Luis where he would hold their visita.[21] Governor Diego de Rebolledo began the visita of San Luis de Xinaica on January 22. In the council house of San Luis there appeared before Governor Rebolledo, Francisco Luis, cacique of San Luis; Antonio García, Captain of San Luis; Antonio de Inija, principal of the same; Pedro García, principal of San Luis; Geronimo, cacique of Abaslaco, in the jurisdiction of San Luis; Francisco, cacique of San Francisco;

---

[20] Ibid.

[21] Ibid.

and the principal men of the caciques.[22]

The Indians indicated that they had no complaint to make about the province lieutenant, Antonio de Sertucha, and his company of soldiers, for they had been treated well by the military. Once again the soldiers appeared in a favorable light, but curiously the Indians had a grievance to present against the Franciscan friars. The caciques acknowledged that sometimes the padres came to their villages and requisitioned laborers without consulting with them. They directed the governor's attention to the fact that this worked a hardship on the village, for their indiscriminant selection of Indians included individuals whose duties were essential to the economic livelihood of the community. Accordingly, the caciques requested that the Franciscans use their vassals only with the prior knowledge and supervision of the pueblo caciques and principal men. Without this supervision, the padres

---

[22]Vicita del lugar de San Luis [de Xinaica], January 22, 1657, Stet. Coll. Escrib. de Cam., Leg. 155, p. 13. San Luis was located approximately 89 leagues west from St. Augustine. See Lucy L. Wenhold (trans.), "A 17th Century Letter of Gabriel Díaz Vara Calderón," p. 8. This undoubtedly corresponded to the term San Luis de Talimali, the name on the list.

assumed unwarranted authority over the Indians. Ulti-
mately, they feared that such actions would undermine the
authority of the village elders. The caciques and principal men further demonstrated the arbitrary nature of the
frairs when they protested about the type and manner of
punishment to which the padres subjected some of the Indians. They beseeched the governor to order a civil investigation of all charges levied against Indians. They
further requested to be informed about such procedures.
In the event that the investigations rendered a decision
against the accused, the caciques requested the right to
supervise the execution of the sentence.[23] The caciques
sought by this attempt to maintain the right to discipline
their own people.

Following what appears to be a pattern, the
caciques agreed that they had voluntarily given food to
the soldiers. Friar Martín de Villanueva and Friar
Bartolome de Vergara, former priests in the village, had
tried to put an end to this practice. They scolded the

---

[23]Vicita del lugar de San Luis [de Xinaica], January 22, 1657, Stet. Coll. Escrib. de Cam., Leg. 155, pp.
13-14.

Indians, whipped Antonio García, a principal man of San
Luis, and indicated a desire to drown Francisco Luis, the
cacique. Cacique Francisco revealed another unpleasant
situation that had occurred with the Franciscans. Father
Juan de Paredes, who had served in the area, wanted the
Indians to carry a cargo of corn and beans and the contents of a church and convent to Santa Helena de
Machava.[24] The Indians, the cacique affirmed, would
have had to perform this service had not the lieutenant
asserted his authority to prevent it. The Indians also
charged that the padre who currently served the village
congregation on one occasion had broken the cooking dishes
for the ridiculous reason that the Indians cooked too
slowly.[25]

On the basis of this accepted testimony which goes
from the sublime to the ridiculous, several possibilities
clearly emerge. There is no defense for Governor

---

[24]Santa Helena de Machaba, a Timucua pueblo, was
located approximately 69 leagues west from St. Augustine.
See Lucy L. Wennold (trans.), "A 17th Century Letter of
Gabriel Díaz Vara Calderón," p. 8.

[25]Vicita del lugar de San Luis [de Xinica], January
22, 1657, Stet. Coll. Escrib. de Cam., Leg. 155, pp. 14-
16.

Rebolledo in the assertion that the Indians deceived him,
for the pattern had appeared too obviously in the preced-
ing investigations of Santa María de Bacuqua and San Pedro
de Patali. The evidence collected consistently praised
the soldiers and was critical of the friars. There is the
possibility that the Indians were afraid to criticize the
soldiers to the governor. One point becomes increasingly
clear--either the governor was attempting to exonerate his
responsibility for the 1656 rebellion, or his ability as
an investigator is suspect.

The Indians declared to Governor Rebolledo that the
military had not forced them to carry any cargoes. When
the frigates arrived from Havana they sometimes helped to
load and unload the cargo. While most crews paid the
Indians for their services, others, contrary to their
promises, did not. The Indians did not consider this a
serious problem, but wished the governor to know about it
so he could rectify it. The caciques described the favorable reaction of the Apalachees to the news of Governor
Rebolledo's decision to increase the size of the garrison
in the province and construct a fort at St. Marks for
their protection. They declared that this was pleasing

for it would provide the necessary protection for Apalachee from the English who had come to their province two years earlier and whom they feared might return again. The Indians indicated that the soldiers would also act as a deterrent to raids by neighboring heathen Indians.[26]

The Indians were not the only ones interested in Governor Rebolledo's military plans. According to this visita the Franciscans also held an interest, but for reasons quite different from those of the Indians. The governor heard Antonio García's account of a conversation with a friar. The Franciscan told García that he had heard of Governor Rebolledo's decision to station a stronger garrison in Apalachee and to construct a fortress at the principal port. The Father told the principal man that it seemed to him that the best location upon which to construct it was on the coast nine leagues west. The padre's argument centered around the fact that because this coastal site was not arable due to the swampy terrain, that the fortress would not stand on vital farming land. Yet, the garrison could provide adequate

---

[26] Ibid.

protection for the port. The site to which the Father referred was St. Marks.[27] The padre took pains in pointing
out to García that if the governor constructed the fort on
the coast and wished to provide an adequate defense for
the province it would be necessary to establish three additional strongholds in strategic areas of Apalachee.
Only such a defensive system could insure protection
against inland enemy raids.[28] In essence, the friar
pointed out that unless the entire province was protected
the fort at St. Marks was superfluous in the fact that it
offered protection for a very restricted area. In other
words, the friar held that there should be four forts or
none.[29]

---

[27] Ibid. See also Lucy L. Wenhold, "The First Fort
of San Marcos de Apalachee," F.H.Q., XXXIV (April, 1956),
p. 301. Captain García went on to say that "it appeared
to Cacique Francisco Luis and the principal men of San
Luis, the village closest to the sea, that the most convenient thing was to place the fort in the part of Apalachee from which the soldiers could respond most readily to
an emergency when needed." The fort proposed by Governor
Rebolledo was not constructed at St. Marks until 1680.

[28] Vicita del lugar de San Luis [de Xinica], January
22, 1657, Stet. Coll. Escrib. de Cam., Leg. 155, pp. 14-
16.

[29] Ibid.

As in the pattern of the other visitas, the caciques and principal men declared that they knew of no
murders, disputes, disturbance or concubinages in their
villages. They were quick to acknowledge that their vassals maintained the proper respect for them. Governor
Rebolledo, pleased with village conditions, gave a set of
instructions and pronounced the visita concluded.[30] Having concluded the inspection, the governor traveled to
San Juan de Aspalaga.

In the pueblo San Juan de Aspalaga there appeared
before Governor Rebolledo, Alonso, cacique of the village;
Manuel, cacique of Pensacola; Jpobal, cacique of Sabe;
Santiago, the heredero of the caciques of Jipe and the
principal men of these caciques. The Indians informed
the governor that they had obeyed the province lieutenant,
and that the soldiers had not mistreated them. In return
for good treatment, the Indians had voluntarily provided
food to the garrison. While the Indians extolled the
goodness of the soldiers, they again felt constrained to

---

[30]Vicita del lugar de San Luis [de Xinica], January
22, 1657, Stet. Coll. Escrib. de Cam., Leg. 155, pp. 14-
16.

present grievances against the friars. This did not con-
stitute a blanket indictment for the Indians pointed out
to Governor Rebolledo the great affection and esteem which
they had had for Father Bernardo de Santa María. Father
Santa María apparently had treated them kindly and had
permitted the Indians to perform many of their ceremonial
dances in the council house. Such was no longer the case.
The Indians informed the governor that Father Santa
María's successor had not treated them as kindly. As a
matter of fact, he had treated them ignominiously. They
referred to one occasion when they assembled to dance.
The padre had taken a heavy stick and had beaten a principal man named Feliciano, the brother-in-law of the cacique
of San Luis, on the back until the stick broke. In an
angered tone the Indians continued to describe the
Franciscans' outrageous conduct. They said that he even
kicked cacique Alonso "punta a pies." These actions
alarmed the dancers, and they fled from the Council House
to avoid similar treatment. In the same vein, the Indians
apprised Governor Rebolledo of another grievance against
the friar. An Indian had been assigned to carry a vessel
to the village of Arapaja in the neighboring province of

Timucua. Illness prevented him from performing his duty; consequently, another Indian was selected to take his place. When the padre came to San Juan de Aspalaga, he learned that the Indian first selected had not performed the task. Without attempting to learn whether the task had been performed or not by others, he ordered the Indian whipped. The flogging which the Indian received was so severe that his back was a bloody mess. The Indians strongly asserted that they were not slaves and should not have to submit to such indignities. They especially resented this treatment because they were Christians and had obeyed all the Father's orders. Therefore, they requested Governor Rebolledo to put an end to this practice.[31]

The cacique and principal men knew of no murders, feuds, or disputes among their subjects, or whether any of their vassals had kept concubines. The caciques' testimony revealed that generally their subjects acted respectfully and obeyed the commands and orders given to them.

---

[31]Vicita del lugar de San Juan de Aspalaga, January 22, 1657, Stet. Coll. Escrib. de Cam., Leg. 155, p. 17. San Juan de Aspalaga was located 78 leagues west from St. Augustine. See Lucy L. Wenhold (trans.), "A 17th Century Letter of Gabriel Díaz Vara Calderón," p. 8.

Alonso, the principal cacique, pointed out that the principal men in his village did not always obey him. Governor
Rebolledo heard his statement and ordered the principal
men to obey Alonso in order to preserve tranquility in the
village. Furthermore, he ordered the Indians to continue
to assist the Father who provided spiritual guidance for
them.[32]

Governor Rebolledo asked the caciques and principal
men if they had heard about his decision to increase the
size of the garrison in the province to afford added protection from the heathen Indians and from the English,
both of whom raided the province from time to time. Both
caciques and principal men replied that it pleased them
to have a squadron of soldiers for defensive purposes.
Governor Rebolledo provided the Indians with a set of
regulations to observe, as he had done to the other
pueblos, and departed from the village.[33]

The visita officials conducted their next investigation in the village of San Martín de Tomoli on January

---

[32] Ibid., pp. 17-18.

[33] Ibid., pp. 18-19.

23, 1657.  There appeared before the visitador Antonio
Hinija, who governed the village in the absence of a head
cacique; Bernardo, cacique of Cibar; Diego, cacique of
San Diego; Bernardo, cacique of Samache and the principal
men of these caciques.  The assembled tribal leaders noted
that few soldiers ever came to their village but, consistent with the pattern, they praised the treatment they
received from the soldiers.  The Indians told Governor
Rebolledo that they had cultivated an agricultural plot
to provide sustenance for Father Juan de Paredes.  Any excess production was given to Indians who had need of it
and for the consumption by individuals who worked on the
convent building for the Franciscans.  It was used also
as food for those who had the duty of cultivating the
field for the friar the following year.  They testified
that there had been a good harvest and the granary had
been filled.  The Indians, however, did not benefit from
the good harvest, for the padre had shipped most of the
food out of the province.  To add insult to injury, he
required the Indians to carry the food to the dock for
him without pay.  As a result, many of the Indians went
hungry and did not have sufficient seed to plant the

friar's field the next spring. Accordingly, they asked

Governor Rebolledo to prevent such actions. The Indians

asked the governor also to permit them to perform their

ceremonial dances and to play the ball game. They noted

with regret that the Franciscans had seen fit to prohibit

ceremonial dancing. Governor Rebolledo took cognizance

of their petition. He issued the same regulations which

he had given to other villages and ordered the Indians to

observe them. The fourth section of the regulations

granted the Indians permission to perform their inof-

fensive ceremonial dances.[34]

On February 5, 1657, Governor Rebolledo inspected

the village San Joseph de Ocuya. He was met by Benito

Ruíz, the cacique of San Joseph; Gaspar, cacique of

Sabacola; Santiago, cacique of Ajapasca; and Juanimo,

the cacique of Chali. All of these caciques were sub-

ordinates of Benito Ruíz. The principal men of the

caciques were also present. As usual the caciques and

---

[34]Vicita del lugar de San Martín de Tomoli, January
23, 1657, Stet. Coll. Escrib. de Cam., Leg. 155, pp. 6-7.
San Martín de Tomoli was located 90 leagues west from St.
Augustine. See Lucy L. Wenhold (trans.), "A 17th Century
Letter of Gabriel Díaz Vara Calderón," p. 9.

principal men testified that they had no complaints about
the military who had been stationed in the province.  Once
again they indicated that the soldiers had treated them
well and in return the Indians had freely provided food to
the military.  The caciques mentioned that their subjects
always maintained the proper respect for them.  They admitted to no knowledge of criminal activity in their villages and knew of no one who kept a concubine or who lived
a scandalous public life.[35]

According to the pattern established in the visita,
after praising the behavior of the soldiers, the Indians
then presented a grievance against the local friar.  In
this instance, they were critical of Friar Miguel Sánchez,
who had served in San Joseph, and who had taken part of
the harvest and had exchanged it for ornaments and items
needed for the convent.  They complained that while their
produce had disappeared, the expected ornaments had not
appeared.  They recognized the need for church fixtures,

---

[35]Vicita de San Joseph de Ocuya, February 5, 1657,
Stet. Coll. Escrib. de Cam., Leg. 155, pp. 20-22.  San
Joseph de Ocuya was located approximately 80 leagues west
from St. Augustine.  See Lucy L. Wenhold (trans.), "A 17th
Century Letter of Gabriel Díaz Vara Calderón," p. 8.

but the friar's unilateral action had left them without
seed to sow the convent's field.[36]

The oppressive character of Friar Sánchez was
further demonstrated in the visita by virtue of testimony
presented by the Indians that the same friar forced them
to bring Cacique Gaspar to the village church when he
failed to attend mass.  Without further investigation,
the Father brutally whipped the cacique, ignorant of the
fact that he had not attended church because of illness.
Because all the village inhabitants knew that Cacique
Gaspar had been ill, they deplored the fact that the
Father had publicly humiliated the chief.  The governor
listened intently as the Indians bemoaned the fact that
the Father had not consulted them or given them the
chance to take the necessary measures to insure that
Gaspar fulfilled his obligations and attended mass.  The
caciques had complained about this matter to the Father
Provincial, San Antonio, when he visited the village.
Although the Provincial assured the Indians that he would

---

[36]Vicita de San Joseph de Ocuya, February 5, 1657,
Stet. Coll. Escrib. de Cam., Leg. 155, pp. 20-22.

investigate their complaint and take the necessary steps to correct the situation, the Indians informed the governor that Friar Sánchez had informed them of the Provincial's decision to take no action. The caciques now hoped the governor would rectify the situation. They also asked Governor Rebolledo to send a priest to the village to replace Friar Sánchez.[37]

In addition, the Indians requested that they be relieved from carrying burdens to St. Augustine for the friars as had been the custom in the past. Governor Rebolledo assured the Indians that he intended to provide the village with a set of instructions which would correct this and other situations. The interpreter, Diego Salvador, read and explained the aranzes to the assemblage. Prior to concluding the visita of San Joseph, the caciques and principal men expressed their apparent pleasure for Governor Rebolledo's military plans for Apalachee. They promised, if the Spanish built a fort in the province, to assist the soldiers.[38]

---

[37] Ibid.

[38] Ibid.

The following day, Governor Rebolledo conducted the visita of the village of San Francisco de Oconi. Before him there appeared Francisco Martín, cacique of San Francisco; Alonso Martín, cacique of San Miguel; and their principal men. In the same monotonous pattern the Indians described the good treatment they had received from the hands of the soldiers. In fact, the Indians emphasized that the soldiers were so kind to them that they liked to see military units come to their villages. So much good will had been created that the villagers gladly supplied the soldiers with food and lodging. All of the caciques affirmed that there had been no feuds or disputes in their villages which were the first ones in Apalachee to experience the work of the missionaries. Consequently, there were no disputes nor discipline problems. Since the village did not have a priest, the inhabitants asked the governor to send them one to supply their religious needs. They also asked Governor Rebolledo to relieve them from carrying burdens and to provide them with instructions to assist them in maintaining an orderly government. The caciques then told the visitador that they had heard that he intended to increase the size of the garrison.

They indicated their pleasure with his desire to protect
the province.  Governor Rebolledo gave the Indians a set
of instructions to obey and concluded the investigation
of the village.[39]

Governor Rebolledo traveled that same day to the
village Santa María de Ayubali to investigate it.  Cacique
Martín of Santa María, his brother, a principal man of the
same village, and Adrian, cacique of Cutachuba appeared
before Governor Rebolledo.  True to form, the Indians informed the governor that his soldiers had not mistreated
them.  As in the case of the other villages, the Indians
affirmed that they had provided food for the soldiers.
The caciques mentioned that tranquility existed in their
villages as they tried to fulfill their obligations as
loyal subjects of the Crown and the church.  Consistent
with the testimony of other villages, the Indians expressed their full pleasure with Governor Rebolledo's decision to increase the size of the Apalachee garrison,

---

[39]Vicita del lugar de San Francisco de Oconi,
February 6, 1657, Stet. Coll. Escrib. de Cam., Leg. 155,
pp. 22-24.  San Francisco de Oconi was located approxi-
mately 77 leagues west from St. Augustine.  See Lucy L.
Wenhold (trans.), "A 17th Century Letter of Gabriel Díaz
Vara Calderón," p. 8.

for it furnished protection against the English and the
heathen Indians. Governor Rebolledo gave them a list of
aranzes and concluded his inspection of the pueblo.[40]

On February 7, 1657, the governor arrived at San
Lorenzo de Ibitachuco to carry out another visita. In
the council house, Don Luis, cacique of the pueblo;
Andrés, cacique of San Juan; Pedro Munoz, cacique of San
Pablo; Thomas, cacique of San Nicolas; Fabían, cacique of
Ajapasca; Lorenzo Moreno, Captain; and Francisco and
Santiago, principal men of Ajapasca met Rebolledo. Once
again, the Indian leaders presented no complaints about
the military, for the soldiers had treated them kindly,
and the Indians had reciprocated this good treatment by
provisioning the soldiers. In fact, the caciques doubted
that an instance had occurred where the military had mistreated the Indians in Apalachee. The caciques and
principal men added that they had looked forward to the

---

[40]Vicita del lugar de Santa María de Ayubali,
February 6, 1657, Stet. Coll. Escrib. de Cam., Leg. 155,
pp. 24-25. Santa María de Ayubali was located approximately 76 leagues west from St. Augustine. Santa María
does not appear on the 1657 list, but La Concepcion de
Ayubali does. See Lucy L. Wenhold (trans.), "A 17th
Century Letter of Gabriel Díaz Vara Calderón," p. 8.

arrival of soldiers, for not only did they provide defense, but they were shining examples of good Christians.
When the tired and hungry soldiers came to their villages,
they provided food and shelter for them, and if the Indians did not have food enough in their own storehouses,
they got it from the convent. This practice, which had
been encouraged in the past by Friar Pedro Muñez, now
brought the Indians and the military into conflict, because the present friar, Antonio de la Cruz, had not encouraged good relations with the military. Father Cruz
had prevented them from providing food and lodging for
the soldiers. The caciques mentioned that they had desired to repair the Royal Highway in the area for the
benefit of the soldiers but that Father Cruz refused to
grant the necessary permission. Father Cruz had justified his position with the excuse that the Indians' tools
could not stand up under the strain of construction and
that the soldiers would not replace the broken implements.
The caciques and principal men testified that the soldiers
had always encouraged them to honor and obey the padres
and to assist them because it was their Christian obligation. Accordingly, it seemed that the fathers had been

less than fair in their observations about the military.[41]

This animosity between the soldiers and the friars, and

the fact that the Indians were torn between loyalty to the

Crown and the church, caused them to revolt from time to

time.

The governor was informed that Father Cruz had com-

mitted still another offense. He had punished the princi-

pal men and a principal woman, a relative of Don Luis, for

very little reason. The woman had received an especially

harsh punishment. She was severely lashed and, as a con-

sequence, she was unable to work. In the nearby village

of San Miguel de Asile, Father Cruz threatened the cacique

and his subjects with a beating if they provided a company

of soldiers with more than calabashes and beans. The

Indians did not care for Father Cruz's attitude, for they

did not want to offer clandestine aid to the soldiers.

Passing on to other matters, the tribal leaders reported

that tranquility prevailed in the village. They, too,

---

[41]Vicita del lugar San Lorenzo de Ibitachuco,
February 7, 1657, Stet. Coll. Escrib. de Cam., Leg. 155,
pp. 25-27. San Lorenzo de Ibitachuco was located approxi-
mately 75 leagues west from St. Augustine. See Lucy L.
Wenhold (trans.), "A 17th Century Letter of Gabriel Díaz
Vara Calderón," p. 8.

were pleased at the prospect of having a fort in the province for defensive purposes. They reminded the governor that they had asked him in the past to increase the size of the Apalachee garrison. Having a garrison was all well and good, but the Indians felt it would serve no useful purpose if Governor Rebolledo later reduced it to please the Franciscans as had happened before. Only the soldiers and not the friars could offer them protection. Governor Rebolledo then gave the caciques and principal men the usual set of aranzes and concluded the inspection of San Lorenzo.[42]

At the village San Miguel de Asile the governor held a short visita. There appeared before him, Gaspar, cacique of the village; Lucas, a cacique; Juan de Medina, principal heir of cacique Lazaro, father of the cacique of Sabe; and the principal men of these pueblos. They stated to the governor that they had no complaint to make about the military. They noted that their vassals lived well with one another, and the governor provided them a

_____

[42]Vicita del lugar de San Lorenzo de Ibitachuco, February 7, 1657, Stet. Coll. Escrib. de Cam., Leg. 155, pp. 25-27.

list of instructions, ending thereby the visita of the village and province.[43]

On February 10, 1657, Governor Rebolledo issued an edict for Apalachee. The auto stipulated that within fifteen days all male and female Timucuan Indians who happened to be in Apalachee province had to return to their homes. Those who did not comply with the mandate would be given a hundred lashes and four years of forced labor in the presidio at St. Augustine. Women would only be lashed. To insure that the order was expedited immediately, one provision of the auto provided that the caciques and principal men would be punished for their failure to enforce the regulations. Apparently Governor Rebolledo issued this ordinance to minimize contacts between the Timucuans and the Apalachees. He was aware of the fact that the rebellion of 1656 had started in Timucua, and he knew that the Apalachee Indians had played only a minor

---

[43]Vicita del lugar de San Miguel de Asile, February 8, 1657, Stet. Coll. Escrib. de Cam., Leg. 155, pp. 29-30. San Miguel de Asile, a Timucuan pueblo, was located approximately 73 leagues west from St. Augustine. See Lucy L. Wenhold (trans.), "A 17th Century Letter of Gabriel Díaz Vara Calderón," p. 8.

part in the uprising. Indicative of this was the fact
that eleven Timucuan Indians had been executed, while no
Apalachees received capital punishment. The governor
ordered that the decree be posted at the council house of
San Lorenzo de Ibitachuco.[44] Having concluded the
Apalachee inspection, Rebolledo prepared to investigate
Timucua.

Governor Rebolledo traveled from San Lorenzo de
Ibitachuco to San Pedro de Potohiriba to begin the visita
of Timucua Province. There, on February 13, 1657, the
governor issued an auto. The visitador noted that he had
come to Timucua to investigate the uprising that had been
perpetrated by some of the caciques, to punish the guilty
ones according to the seriousness of their crime, and to
conduct a thorough investigation in the area. Because the
visita of Apalachee had required so much time, Rebolledo
dispatched Captain Matheo Luis de Florencia to the
Timucuan villages to tell the caciques and principal men
to come to San Pedro de Potohiriba where he intended to

---

[44]Bando que publico por la Procincia de Apalache,
February 10, 1657, Stet. Coll. Escrib. de Cam., Leg. 155,
pp. 30-31.

conduct the province's investigation. Governor Rebolledo
ordered the Indians to assemble in one place because of
the great distance between the Timucuan villages and also
because all of them were not located on the Royal Highway.[45]

On February 13, 1657, in compliance with the governor's auto, there assembled in the council house at San
Pedro de Potohiriba, Diego Jeba, principal cacique of the
village; María Meléndez, cacica of Santa Aña; Lazaro,
cacique of Chamile and San Martín; Francisco, cacique of
Cachipile; Lorenzo, cacique of Chuaguine; Alonso Patrana,
principal cacique of Arapaja and Santa Fé; Domingo,
cacique of San Francisco Potano; Francisco Alonzo, cacique
of San Pablo; Juan Bauptista, cacique of San Juan; Pedro
Meléndez, cacique of Santa Elena de Machaba; Sebastían,
cacique of San Joseph; Dionicio, cacique of San Lorenzo;
Sebastían, cacique of San Matheo; Francisco, cacique of
San Francisco; Francisco Alonso, cacique of San Miguel;
Francisco Lucas, cacique of San Lucas; Santiago, cacique
of San Matheo; Domingo, cacique of San Augustin; and

---

[45] Auto, February 13, 1657, Stet. Coll. Escrib. de
Cam., Leg. 155, pp. 31-33.

Lucía, cacica of Nihoica. Diego Salvador, who had served
as Governor Rebolledo's interpreter in Apalachee, rendered
his services also in Timucua.[46]

The interpreter read the auto para la vicita to the
Indians and explained that Governor Rebolledo had come to
the province to investigate the causes of the rebellion,
and to listen to any complaints or grievances which the
Timucuans had to offer. He wanted to know especially if
the Indians obeyed their tribal leaders, if there existed
any enmity among the villages, if any murders had occurred, if any Indian kept a concubine, or if the soldiers
had mistreated the Indians in any way. Diego Jeba was the
first to speak. He informed Rebolledo that he had served
as the cacique of San Pedro de Potohiriba for only a short
time, and that he could not answer most of these questions. At the same time, he informed the governor that
it might behoove him to confirm the rights of Francisco

---

[46] Vicita del lugar de San Pedro [de Potohiriba] y
demas caciques de Ustaca [Timucua], February 13, 1657,
Stet. Coll. Escrib. de Cam., Leg. 155, pp. 33-34. San
Pedro de Potohiriba was located approximately 67 leagues
west from St. Augustine. See Lucy L. Wenhold (trans.),
"A 17th Century Letter of Gabriel Díaz Vara Calderón,"
p. 8.

to the caciqueship of San Francisco which Governor Rebolledo agreed to do. The cacique of Chamile, Lazaro, told
the visitador that he intended to relocate his village at
San Martín. In view of this anticipated move, he asked
Governor Rebolledo to prohibit any Indians from occupying
Chamile and illicitly requisitioning the food in the storage bins while he was engaged in the removal. The cacique
of Arapaja and Santa Fé supported Lazaro's request. Pedro
Meléndez, principal cacique of Santa Helena de Machaba informed the governor that Dionicio, cacique of San Lorenzo,
one of his subordinates, had refused to obey his orders
and had attempted to build a following and usurp his position. The visitador dealt with this complaint by ordering
Cacique Dionicio to render allegiance to Pedro Meléndez.
All of the caciques and principal men had no complaints
about the soldiers. Governor Rebolledo provided the assembled tribal leaders with a set of instructions to observe which the interpreter read and explained to them.
The visitador ordered the caciques to repair the roads in
the province and to build bridges over creeks and streams
in order to expedite travels between the villages. Rebolledo noted that this would facilitate easier mobility for

the couriers and padres. The caciques agreed to carry out the instructions.[47]

On the same day there appeared before Governor Rebolledo in the council house, Martín, cacique of San Pedro de Aquatiro and Alexo, cacique of Santa María. They told the visitador that they had no complaints to make about anything or anyone and the governor concluded his inspection of Timucua. He provided the caciques with a set of rules to observe and prepared to return to St. Augustine.[48]

---

[47]Vicita del lugar de San Pedro [de Potohiriba] y demas caciques de Ustaca [Timucua], February 13, 1657, Stet. Coll. Escrib. de Cam., Leg. 155, pp. 34-35.

[48]Otra Vicita [San Pedro de Potohiriba], February 13, 1657, Stet. Coll. Escrib. de Cam., Leg. 155, p. 36.

# CHAPTER IV

## REBOLLEDO AND THE FRANCISCANS:

## CHARGE AND COUNTERCHARGE

Governor Diego de Rebolledo concluded his general
inspection of western Florida at the Timucuan village of
San Pedro de Potohiriba on February 13, 1657, and departed
for St. Augustine soon afterwards. The 1656 rebellion,
which the Timucuans precipitated, was over, for Spanish
soldiers, commanded by Sergeant-Major Adrian de Cañicares,
had moved quickly to crush the uprising. Governor Rebolledo returned to the capital convinced that he had sufficient evidence to prove that the Timucuans rose up in
rebellion because the Franciscans mistreated them. The
testimony which the Indians gave during the course of the
visita certainly did nothing to detract from the governor's belief. Without fail, the village caciques and
their subjects swore that the soldiers always treated them
with kindness. And equally consistent, they never devi-
ated from their testimony that the Franciscans abused

them. On the surface at least, Governor Rebolledo had ample facts to absolve his administration of any blame for the Timucuan rebellion. The testimony of the Indians, recorded by Juan Moreno y Segovia, the scribe, appeared conclusive that the Franciscans, who exercised disruptive influences in the provinces, caused the Timucuans to revolt. Governor Rebolledo had the necessary documents to justify his administration before the Council of the Indies. In essence, the visita proceedings seemed to vindicate him from any responsibility for the rebellion. The blame for the revolt apparently rested with the friars not the soldiers.

On May 8, 1657, Sergeant-Major Adrian de Cañicares wrote to Governor Rebolledo to report on the state of affairs in Apalachee. The Sergeant-Major revealed that the Franciscan Father Provincial, Francisco de San Antonio, came to the province shortly after the governor's departure. Cañicares mentioned in his letter that the Father Provincial acted in a peculiar manner. Anxious to find out the reason for his strange behavior, the Sergeant-Major asked the soldiers if they had any information. He learned that the Father Provincial had in his possession

letters written by a friar and an Indian of Timucua.  The
soldiers had no information about the contents of the letters.  They told the Sergeant-Major that the Father Provincial exercised great care when he talked to them and
never did he mention the letters.  Sergeant-Major Cañicares suspected that the letters contained valuable information, and he determined to question the Father Provincial about them.  Cañicares approached Father San
Antonio soon afterwards and asked the Provincial if he
had any news from Timucua.  Father San Antonio acknowledged that he received two letters but refused to reveal
the contents of them.  The Father Provincial then directed
the conversation to Apalachee affairs.  He admitted to
Cañicares that on the surface tranquility prevailed in
the province, but he insinuated the probability of events
developing to disturb the calm.  Father San Antonio's
subtle suggestion of another Indian uprising disturbed
the Sergeant-Major.  The Sergeant-Major expressed his
opinion to the governor that the Franciscans acted more
often than not as obstructionists in Apalachee.  Especially did it appear that the friars tried to turn the
Indians against the soldiers, hoping thereby to get the

garrison withdrawn from the province.[1]

Sergeant-Major Cañicares pointed out that the Franciscans concentrated their nefarious efforts on Cacique Martín,[2] who tended to go along with an apparent scheme to get rid of the soldiers. The friars prevailed on the cacique to discuss with Don Luís whether there existed a need for soldiers in the province. Cacique Martín agreed to present the matter to Don Luís, but he pointed out to the friars that the Apalachee caciques generally endorsed the San Luís cacique's opinions, since he represented the largest village in the province. Don Luís expressed his pleasure to Martín not only at having a garrison, but also for Governor Rebolledo's decision to increase it to the size where it provided protection for the Indians. Having failed to influence Don Luís, Cacique Martín altered his tactics. He informed the Sergeant-Major that a food

---

[1]Sergeant-Major Adrian de Cañicares to Governor Rebolledo, May 8, 1657, Stet. Coll. Escrib. de Cam., Leg. 155, pp. 51-52.

[2]Ibid. The cacique's name was not mentioned in the document but the reference probably was to Cacique Martín of Guaca who had served as the spokesman during the visitas of Santa María de Bacuqua. See vicita del lugar [Santa María] de Bacuqua, January 19, 1657, Stet. Coll. Escrib. de Cam., Leg. 155, p. 9.

shortage existed in Apalachee, especially in his village, Santa María de Bacuqua. The cacique asserted that Governor Rebolledo granted him permission, when he conducted the visita, to relocate his village because the fields produced poor harvests. In addition, Martín observed that the dislocation caused in changing village sites interfered with the planting of crops, and the Indians did not have a bountiful harvest. The cacique mentioned only soil sterility and village relocations as the causal factors for the food shortage. Martín did not suggest that discontent, caused by the Timucuan rebellion, exercised any influence on the situation. He was quick to admit that the Indians intended to provide food for the soldiers, but he expressed his opinion that since there was a food shortage a reduction from twelve to six infantrymen was in order. A reduced number, Martín felt, would prevent placing undue hardship on any village. Perhaps in an attempt to provide additional cover for his subtlety, the cacique told Cañicares that the Apalachees intended to construct a new barracks for the garrison.[3]

---

[3] Sergeant-Major Adrian de Cañicares to Governor

In spite of the fact that Don Luís spoke favorably
of the increase in the size of the garrison, the Sergeant-
Major did not feel relief. He knew that the San Luís
cacique exerted more influence than any other cacique in
the province, but the Franciscan intrigues with Cacique
Martín and the fact that he requested a reduction in the
number of soldiers bothered the Sergeant-Major. He
wondered if other Apalachee caciques felt the same as
Cacique Martín. The peculiar conduct of the Father Provincial continued to haunt him, and he decided that it
was necessary to learn the views of the other village
caciques on this matter. If the potential existed for a
rebellion, as the Provincial indicated, the Sergeant-Major
determined to discover it and put an end to it. It was
imperative, he felt, to preserve order in the province.
The government had been fortunate in 1656 as only the
Timucuans revolted. The prospect of the Apalachees ris-
ing in arms and enticing the Timucuans to join them was

---

Rebolledo, May 8, 1657, Stet. Coll. Escrib. de Cam., Leg.
155, pp. 51-52.

not a pleasant thought to consider.[4]

Sergeant-Major Cañicares waited until the Father Provincial departed for St. Augustine before he set out to confer with the village caciques. Once again the caciques followed faithfully the pattern which developed during Rebolledo's visita. They affirmed that they enjoyed good relations with the soldiers and expressed their pleasure with the governor's decision to increase the size of the garrison. In addition, the Sergeant-Major found no evidence of the discontent which the Provincial suggested might give rise to rebellion. He concluded that Father San Antonio hinted the possibility of an uprising because the Franciscans earnestly wished to cause difficulty for the soldiers and the governor. Cañicares concluded that the friars probably were jealous, because Cacique Luís did not speak out against the presence of a garrison in the province or an increase in the size of it. No doubt the friars detested the good relations which the soldiers enjoyed with all of the Apalachee villages, for they

---

[4] Sergeant-Major Adrian de Cañicares to Governor Rebolledo, May 21, 1657, Stet. Coll. Escrib. de Cam., Leg. 155, pp. 52-53.

apparently felt that the military undermined their influence among the Indians. The Sergeant-Major expressed his belief to Governor Rebolledo that the Franciscans had some type of scheme afoot to thwart the governor's military objectives in the province and to get the soldiers withdrawn. Apparently, the friar's efforts to influence Cacique Martín constituted a beginning which portended a good deal of difficulty for the military and warranted the closest observation. The Sergeant-Major regretted that the Franciscans chose to work at cross-purposes to the military in the province. It was essential for the church and the Crown to cooperate, because the religious and military needs of Apalachee were significant. The jealousy which the Fathers apparently reflected served no useful purpose at all.[5]

Sergeant-Major Cañicares' report received important support when Adjutant Pedro de la Puerta wrote to Governor Rebolledo on July 12, 1657. The Adjutant also expressed the opinion that the Franciscans opposed the presence of

---

[5] Adjutant Pedro de la Puerta to Governor Rebolledo, July 12, 1657, Stet. Coll. Escrib. de Cam., Leg. 155, p. 54.

the military in Apalachee. He informed the governor of
discussions with the friars in which they insinuated that
if Governor Rebolledo persisted in his determination to
maintain the garrison at twelve strong and to construct
a fortress at St. Marks that the Indians' discontent would
be such that they would rise up in rebellion. Puerta commented also on the distasteful activities of the Father
Provincial in the province. He agreed with Cañicares that
Father San Antonio acted strangely after his arrival from
Timucua, and that the Provincial was bent on creating
problems for the soldiers. Apparently, Father San Antonio
had come to western Florida not for the purpose of survey-
ing the religious needs of the missions, but to conduct an
investigation of the military. Not only did the Provincial do this, but he also went among the Indians and
encouraged them to complain about the soldiers, so that
they would be withdrawn from Apalachee. This type of
action, the Adjutant declared, reflected conduct unbecom-
ing to a priest. Puerta admitted that he knew Father San
Antonio's assertions of the soldiers mistreating the Indians were false. In a spirit of fairness he determined to
investigate them thoroughly to see if the soldiers treated

the Indians badly. The Adjutant conducted an investigation, and his findings matched those of the Sergeant-Major. The Indians swore that the soldiers never abused them, but that the friars on occasion had done so. In addition, Puerta found no evidence of the discontent which the Provincial indicated. There was no evidence at all to implicate the military of misconduct.[6]

Adjutant Puerta suggested that the Franciscans were jealous of the soldiers because the Indians liked them. They deplored the fact that the Indians voluntarily gave food and lodging to the soldiers when they came to their villages. Evidently this jealousy had reached the point where the friars earnestly wished the soldiers to commit an indiscreet act so they could report it to the Crown. By this means they hoped to achieve a dual purpose. Such an act on the part of the soldiers might cause the Crown to order their withdrawal from the province and mean that Governor Rebolledo had no chance to fulfill his defensive plans for the province. Puerta noted that the friars constantly pleaded with the Indians to get them to say that

---

[6]Ibid.

the soldiers mistreated them. The Adjutant admitted that all of the Franciscans did not oppose the presence of the military, for apparently some understood the reason for the garrison and the increase in the size of it. Two friars, however, represented themselves as archtypes among the opposing priests. Father Alonso del Moral, in particular, did his best to excite the Indians and to turn them against the soldiers. The other mischievous Franciscan lived not in Apalachee but in Timucua. Father Bamba, of Santa Helena de Machaba, the Adjutant discovered, exercised such a disruptive influence that it extended past the Timucuan borders to disturb the tranquility of Apalachee. Such priests, Puerta observed, served only a harmful purpose. They had only their own selfish interest at heart, and deserved to be recalled from the province.[7]

On July 18, 1657, Sergeant-Major Cañicares dispatched a second report to Governor Rebolledo. He suggested that tranquility still existed in the province in

---

[7] Sergeant-Major Adrian de Cañicares to Governor Rebolledo, July 18, 1657, Stet. Coll. Escrib. de Cam., Leg. 155, p. 55.

spite of the fact that certain of the Franciscans assidu-
ously endeavored to stir up the Indians and to turn them
against the soldiers. The Timucuan Indians exhibited
signs of restlessness, and there existed a real possibility of another uprising. He insinuated that the
Timucuans probably were more amenable than the Apalachees
to the Franciscan schemes. Sergeant-Major Cañicares assured the governor that he had informed the Apalachee
caciques of a shipment of wool which Rebolledo intended
to send them for clothing purposes. The Indians, he
noted, were grateful for the governor's generosity.
Cañicares informed Governor Rebolledo that a recent injury had impeded him in the performance of his official
duties. An axe wound in the leg largely confined him to
his bed. The wound became infected, and he suffered from
fever periodically. The Sergeant-Major regretted that
his injury rendered him virtually useless to the Royal
Service at such a critical time when the Franciscans appeared determined to cause the soldiers as much difficulty
as possible.[8]

[8]Ibid.

On August 4, 1657, Father Provincial Francisco de San Antonio, Friar Juan de Medina, Friar Sebastían Martínez, Friar Jacinto Dominquez, Friar Alonso del Moral, and Friar Juan Caldera presented a petition to Governor Rebolledo. The friars pointed out to the governor that they drew up the document in response to a request made by the poor Indians. The Indians were so distressed by Governor Rebolledo's plans for Apalachee that they had turned to the Fathers for help. Specifically, the Indians did not want Governor Rebolledo to increase the size of the provincial garrison, an action already taken, because the soldiers had mistreated them. Because of the precedent already established, the Apalachees reasoned that more soldiers only meant more abuses. The Indians' statements to the Franciscans sharply differed from the testimony which they had given to Governor Rebolledo when he visited the provinces. The Apalachees, probably out of fear, told the governor what apparently he wished to hear, namely that the soldiers treated them well and the friars abused them. Once Rebolledo left the province, the

Indians expressed quite different sentiments to the Franciscans.[9]

The Franciscans pointed out that the Timucuan rebellion of 1656 and the discontent which spread to Apalachee and still existed there, set back the interests of
the church and Crown in the provinces.  The Timucuans revolted not against the church but against the Crown, because of the intense hostility which they felt toward the
soldiers stationed there.  This hatred resulted because of
the work which the soldiers forced the Indians to do
against their will.  The soldiers, not the Franciscans,
required the Indians to serve as cargo bearers and to
perform all kinds of menial tasks.  In effect, the soldiers reduced the Indians to a point which approximated
slavery.  Continuing to press their case, the friars
vigorously denied that the Franciscan Order entered into

---

[9] [Franciscan] Petición [to Governor Rebolledo],
August 4, 1657, Stet. Coll. Escrib. de Cam., Leg. 155, pp.
37-39.  See also vicita del lugar [Santa María] de
Bacuqua, January 19, 1657, Stet. Coll. Escrib. de Cam.,
Leg. 155, pp. 7-10; Vicita del lugar de San Pedro de
Patali, January 19, 1657, Stet. Coll. Escrib. de Cam.,
Leg. 155, p. 10; Vicita del lugar de San Juan de
Aspalaga, January 22, 1657, Stet. Coll. Escrib. de Cam.,
Leg. 155, pp. 18-19.

the rebellion picture at all, and they insinuated that the only reason which caused the poor Indians to testify, during Rebolledo's visita, against the padres was because they feared further reprisals from the governor. The Indians felt, and with some justification, that Sergeant-Major Cañicares had punished them too severely when he put down the rebellion. The fact that he executed eleven caciques seemed to the Timucuans an extremely harsh retribution. Father Provincial San Antonio had written to the Crown in an effort to make known the terrible state of affairs which existed in the provinces prior to the Timucuan rebellion. These conditions, the Father Provincial pointed out to the King, existed before the appointment of Diego de Rebolledo as governor, but they had reached their nadir during his administration. Unfortunately, the Crown had taken no measures to correct the situation, and the Timucuans revolted. The Franciscans told Governor Rebolledo that they had also dispatched a letter to the Crown protesting his decision to increase the size of the Apalachee garrison. The presence of more soldiers meant more mistreatment of the Indians, and the discontent which the Apalachees reflected would have no chance to abate as

long as the garrison remained large. The friars raised
doubt as to whether any concrete need existed in Apalachee
Province which required twelve soldiers. The Franciscans
readily agreed that the presence of two soldiers and a
commander for observation reasons did not pose serious
problems. Twelve soldiers had no chance to produce anything but hostility among the Apalachees. The soldiers
would require the Apalachees to serve as virtual slaves
for them. As had occurred in Timucua, this situation
might produce another rebellion--a rebellion against the
military rather than the church as was the case in 1656.
The friars concluded their petition on a forceful note.
The mission program in Apalachee had no chance to succeed
at all with a twelve man garrison at San Luís. If the
soldiers remained in Apalachee, the Father Provincial had
no choice other than to recall the friars from the missions.[10]

The following day, August 5, 1657, the public
scribe, Juan Moreno, read the contents of the Franciscan

---

[10] [Franciscan] Petición [to Governor Rebolledo],
August 4, 1657, Stet. Coll. Escrib. de Cam., Leg. 155,
pp. 37-39.

petition to Governor Rebolledo. The friars laid the blame for the 1656 rebellion squarely on Rebolledo's shoulders. The padres challenged the integrity of his administration. Their petition stated boldly that the rebellion resulted because the Indians resented the presence of soldiers not friars, because the soldiers were the ones who abused the Indians. The friars' arguments suggested essentially that Governor Rebolledo had not gathered all of the evidence when he conducted the visita of Apalachee and Timucua.[11] Rebolledo concluded apparently that the Crown might view his visita as an attempt to cover up deficiencies of his administration, for he went to extensive efforts to explain his actions.

The governor replied that the Franciscans began their missionary program in Apalachee as early as the administration of Governor Luis de Horruytiner (1633-1638). He pointed out that Horruytiner's successor, Damían de Vega Castro y Pardo (1638-1645) sent the first contingent of soldiers to Apalachee where they remained

---

[11][Governor Rebolledo's] Notificacíon y Repuesta [to the Franciscans], August 5, 1657, Stet. Coll. Escrib. de Cam., Leg. 155, pp. 40-50.

until Sergeant-Major Pedro Benedit Horruytiner assumed the
governorship in 1648. Horruytiner, who governed for only
a year, recalled the garrison in response to a Franciscan
request. This action left the province without a defensive system. There was no one to administer justice to
the Indians, or to keep an eye on the ships that entered
and departed from the harbor at St. Marks. As a result,
there existed an excellent opportunity for the English or
other foreign powers to establish a base of operation in
the province. When Rebolledo assumed the governorship
(1651) the officials at Havana and St. Augustine urged him
to return a contingency of soldiers to Apalachee. Several
reasons dictated the necessity to maintain troops in the
province. Only the military had the necessary means to
supervise the conduct of the Indians and prevent them from
supplying alien vessels with food in exchange for trade
items. Apparently the Apalachees had resumed their illicit trade after the soldiers had withdrawn. This only
encouraged the enemy to return. In a time of necessity
an additional factor entered the question also--food could
be procured from the Indians and sent to the presidio at
St. Augustine. Most important of all, the presence of a

garrison would thwart any enemy plans to establish a foot-hold at St. Marks--the principal port of Apalachee.[12]

In view of those reasons, Governor Rebolledo decided to send Captain Antonio de Sertucha and two infantrymen to Apalachee as a temporary measure. He concluded that Captain Sertucha had the ability to settle the matters which the Indians customarily brought to St. Augustine for adjudication. This action gave him the opportunity to deal more effectively with problems at St. Augustine and in Guale. Captain Sertucha wasted no time at all once he reached Apalachee. Hampered by an inadequate force of soldiers, he did his best to protect St. Marks against enemy incursions. He was not long in the Apalachee province before he sent word to Governor Rebolledo that a pirate ship had sailed into the harbor at St. Marks and that he needed reinforcements. Governor Rebolledo responded quickly to the call for help and dispatched Captain Gregorio Bravo and thirty soldiers to

---

[12] Ibid. See also Rebolledo to the King, October 18, 1657, in Brooks, The Unwritten History of Old St. Augustine, pp. 102-105. See also Lucy L. Wenhold, "The First Fort of San Marcos de Apalachee," F.H.Q., XXXIV (April, 1954), pp. 301-313.

render assistance. In the meantime, Captain Sertucha summoned the Apalachee Indians together to defend the province against the pirates. The pirates, facing a stiff resistance, departed before Captain Bravo arrived with reinforcements. Since the emergency no longer existed, Bravo obtained a supply of food on his arrival and returned to St. Augustine.[13]

The Apalachee garrison apparently remained at three strong until the Timucuan rebellion of 1656. At that time, the governor decided to put more than an observation team in Apalachee. Factors other than the rebellion influenced his decision. The Apalachees requested that he increase the number of soldiers to furnish protection for them against the English and the heathen Indians. He asserted that the Franciscans in the province asked him to station additional troops in the province. All of these factors influenced his decision to increase the San Luís garrison by ten additional soldiers. The governor took great care in the selection of the Apalachee commandant. He chose Sergeant-Major Adrian de Cañicares y Ossorio

---

[13]Ibid.

because he had served the Crown for a number of years and was an intimate friend of the Franciscans. The Sergeant-Major's primary purpose was to make certain that no alien ships entered St. Marks. Rebolledo gave Cañicares explicit orders to watch the St. Marks area closely because news came to St. Augustine that the English were determined to occupy a position somewhere in the area. Don Diego de Cardenas, Spain's ambassador to England, acquired this information and forwarded it to the Madrid government. Don Juan de Montano, the governor and captain-general of Cuba, gained essentially the same information from captured prisoners who admitted that the English entertained such designs.[14]

Governor Rebolledo marshalled additional facts to bolster his decision to increase the number of soldiers in Apalachee. Powerful enemy fleets appeared off the entrance to the harbor at Havana from time to time, and these squadrons posed potential danger to Apalachee. The governor singled out the English, in particular, as a threat to Florida. Spain had to thwart all English

---

[14]Ibid.

designs in Apalachee because of the potential which the
province possessed as a food producing area. Rebolledo
implied that if the English gained a foothold in Apalachee
they would undermine the Franciscan mission program--a
program which he desired, contrary to Franciscan charges,
to prosper. The governor asserted that he desired to see
the mission activities continue without interference,
hence another factor in his decision to increase the garrison's strength. The Franciscans failed to consider that
St. Augustine was too far away from Apalachee to dispatch
troops in time to ward off an invasion. Still another
factor which he pointed out to the friars was the important fact that St. Marks lay only thirty leagues distant
from the area where the galleons rendezvoused to go to
Havana and from there to Spain. If the English established themselves at St. Marks, this would place them
in a position only six or seven sailing days from Havana.
From this St. Marks vantage point, they could do considerable damage to Spanish shipping in the Gulf of Mexico.[15]

Governor Rebolledo pointed out that a significant

---

[15] Ibid.

reduction had occurred in the Indian population of
Timucua. He concluded that the plague and smallpox were
responsible for the decline. He did not mention the possibility that large numbers of Timucuans had fled from
the province when Sergeant-Major Cañicares arrived to put
down the rebellion. In view of the population decline,
Rebolledo concluded that a recall of some of the friars
from the mission fields was necessary. He saw no need to
keep the priests when no need for their presence existed.
The governor observed that the Franciscans might wish to
extend their mission system beyond the border of Timucua
and Apalachee. In particular, Rebolledo suggested the
Apalachicolas and the Choctaws as Indian groups who unfortunately lived without the benefit of Christian instruction. It seemed reasonable to assign Fathers, not
needed in Timucua, to these Indians who lived without
spiritual guidance.[16]

The governor pointed out an inherent difficulty if
Father Provincial San Antonio decided to send friars to
the Apalachicolas and the Choctaws. Apalachee needed to

---

[16]Ibid.

retain a strong garrison of soldiers and a fort had to be constructed at St. Marks before sending the friars into new areas. The first order of importance was to secure Apalachee against external and internal disorders. Retention of an effective garrison and the erection of a presidio near the sea would aid in solving these problems. It had been difficult to defend Apalachee before the increase in the garrison's strength, and it was not prudent to begin mission programs in the new areas until an adequate base of support was established for them in Apalachee. The governor pointed out that the Apalachicola and Choctaw provinces bordered on Apalachee, and the caciques in these areas requested missionaries during the administration of Governor Benito Ruiz de Salazar Vallecilla (1648-1651). Because of the difficulty of supplying and protecting the padres from St. Augustine, no mission work was attempted among them. Rebolledo indicated his desire, if his plans for Apalachee were not altered, to broaden the program within a reasonable time.[17]

---

[17] Ibid. See also Rebolledo to the King, October 18, 1657, in Brooks, The Unwritten History of Old St. Augustine, pp. 102-105.

Governor Rebolledo challenged the Franciscans' assertion that the Apalachees did not want soldiers in their
province. The Apalachees had not complained to him about
the military when he conducted a visita in the province.
He noted letters which he received from the garrison officers such as Sergeant-Major Cañicares and Adjutant
Puerta did not mention any ill will that the Indians
harbored toward the soldiers. In fact the officers observed that the Indians were pleased that additional soldiers come to Apalachee. Such relations did not prevail
always between the Indians and the friars. The officers
reported that the Franciscans tried to turn the Indians
against the soldiers and they did their best to get the
Indians to complain about the presence of the garrison.
Adjutant Pedro de la Puerta suggested in his report that
the friars, by their behavior, caused the Timucuan Indians to rebel in 1656. The governor observed that Father
Alonso del Moral played a most active role in the Franciscan efforts to disturb the Indians and to thwart,
thereby, any defensive plans which the military had for
the area. Father Moral had not labored alone in his efforts to excite the Indians. The primary reason the

Franciscans wanted the military removed centered around
the fact that the soldiers interfered with their plans for
the province. The Indians liked the soldiers and this
display of esteem made the friars jealous. It appeared
to Governor Rebolledo that the Franciscans wished to exercise absolute control in Apalachee. The Indians providing
food and supplies to the soldiers was interpreted by the
Franciscans in the wrong way. The St. Augustine government had no intention of placing obstacles in the way of
the church. In fact the government wished to help the
friars as much as possible. The province required a
basic defensive system, and there was more to consider in
Apalachee than the special interests of the Franciscans.[18]

Governor Rebolledo observed that the Franciscans on
occasion had acted in an immature manner. Not only had
the friars attempted to undermine the defensive system,

---

[18] [Governor Rebolledo's] Notificacíon y Repuesta
[to the Franciscans], August 5, 1657, Stet. Coll. Escrib.
de Cam., Leg. 155, pp. 40-50; Sergeant-Major Adrian de
Cañicares to Governor Rebolledo, May 8, 1657, Stet. Coll.
Escrib. de Cam., Leg. 155, pp. 51-52; Same to Same, May
21, 1657, Stet. Coll. Escrib. de Cam., Leg. 155, pp. 52-
53; Same to Same, July 18, 1657, Stet. Coll. Escrib. de
Cam., Leg. 155, p. 55; Adjutant Pedro de la Puerta to
Governor Rebolledo, July 12, 1657, Stet. Coll. Escrib.
de Cam., Leg. 155, p. 54.

but some of them had abandoned their responsibilities to the Indians without any reason at all. The decision to send Lieutenant Antonio de Sertucha to Apalachee had precipitated discontent among the Sons of St. Francis. Six of the friars decided thereupon to leave the province, and they sailed for Havana. A storm arose and they drowned. The priests failed to request permission from their prelate to leave which was the normal procedure and simply departed from the mission field. There was no reason for departure except perhaps the Fathers interpreted Lieutenant Sertucha's arrival as the first step in a plan designed to limit their power and influence. No such plan or design existed and Governor Rebolledo pointed out once again that he decided to send Lieutenant Sertucha and two infantrymen to Apalachee after royal officials at Havana and St. Augustine urged him to return troops to the province on a permanent basis. The basic reason behind their request was to prevent alien ships from stopping at St. Marks and conducting illicit trade with the Indians. An unguarded harbor presented an open invitation to foreign powers to establish an outpost in the area. These reasons, and no others, persuaded the governor to return a military force to Apalachee.[19]

Governor Rebolledo mentioned that a large Indian delegation visited him at St. Augustine shortly after he concluded the visita. Cacique Andres of San Juan Lorenzo and twenty-four followers came to the Florida capital to confer with him and other royal officials. The governor, obviously pleased with this apparent display of esteem, took pains to insinuate that the loyalty of these Indians played a major role in the fact that the Apalachees did not join forces with the rebellious Timucuans in 1656. While at the capital the governor furnished lodging for the Indians in his official home. Other Apalachee caciques, he affirmed, also expressed their desire to come to St. Augustine. Not only did the Apalachees come to the capital to confer with the governor, they communicated to him information which they deemed important. Don Luís, an important cacique from San Lorenzo de Ibitachuco, sent

---

[19][Governor Rebolledo's] Notificacíon y Repuesta [to the Franciscans], August 5, 1657, Stet. Coll. Escrib. de Cam., Leg. 155, pp. 40-50; Rebolledo to the King, October 18, 1657, in Brooks, The Unwritten History of Old St. Augustine, pp. 102-105; Lucy L. Wenhold, "The First Fort of San Marcos de Apalachee," F.H.Q., XXXIV (April, 1954), pp. 301-313.

word to Governor Rebolledo that Father Alonso del Moral
and Father Miguel Garcon traveled about the province encouraging him and the other caciques to raise a protest in
order that the soldiers might be withdrawn. Governor
Rebolledo affirmed that he foresaw that these priests
might cause difficulty, and that he asked Father Provincial San Antonio not to send them to Apalachee where
they did so much to stir up difficulty.[20]

The governor made it clear that he did not intend
for anyone, friar or soldier, to mistreat the Indians of
Apalachee. Anxious that the Apalachees understood fully
his position, Governor Rebolledo instructed Adjutant Pedro
la Puerta to keep a close watch on the conduct of the garrison soldiers. He was to investigate any charge by the
Indians that a soldier or priest had mistreated an Indian.
Rebolledo asserted that he made every effort to guarantee
that the Indians did not have to serve as cargo bearers,
but admitted that it was difficult to put an immediate end
to this practice. On one occasion the soldiers asked the

---

[20] [Governor Rebolledo's] Notificacíon y Repuesta
[to the Franciscans], August 5, 1657, Stet. Coll. Escrib.
de Cam., Leg. 155, pp. 40-50.

Indians to help them complete a defensive system at San
Luis, and had no money with which to pay the Indians for
their services when they finished their task. Without a
doubt this caused discontent among the Indians, but the
moment the subsidy arrived from New Spain, Governor Rebolledo sent the treasurer, Joseph de Prado, to pay the Indians for services rendered.[21]

Rebolledo acknowledged that the Spaniards had no
chance to maintain a garrison in Apalachee unless the
Indians cooperated with them. There was no possible way
to construct a fortress at St. Marks without their assistance. It was not enough to have soldiers in Apalachee
or Timucua merely for the purpose of putting down rebellions. From time to time the Indians became excited for
no reason at all, and the soldiers played useful roles in
calming them before an uprising occurred. In addition,
the presence of a strong garrison guaranteed the missionaries some semblance of protection in the event of a rebellion. As a case in point, Governor Rebolledo referred

---

[21]Instrucíon [from Governor Rebolledo for Apala-
chee], August 8, 1657, Stet. Coll. Escrib. de Cam., Leg.
155, pp. 56-58.

to the rebellion of 1646. The cause of the revolt was difficult to determine, for the Indians killed both Fathers and soldiers indiscriminately, and they burned the churches as well. Governor Rebolledo suggested the rebellion flared up because of an insufficient force of soldiers in the province to subdue rebellious tendencies. He concluded that an effective military force was as essential for the province as the friars. The Crown's best interest required the presence of both the friar and the soldier.[22]

Governor Rebolledo observed that the Franciscans vacillated in their attitude toward the soldiers. As a result, no one knew how to regard their statements. The friars had been favorably disposed to the erection of a fort and to the strengthening of the garrison when the Timucuans revolted in 1646. Eleven years later they had changed their minds, although the defensive needs of the province were no less urgent. Governor Rebolledo made it

---

[22] [Governor Rebolledo's] Notificacíon y Repuesta [to the Franciscans], August 5, 1657, Stet. Coll. Escrib. de Cam., Leg. 155, pp. 40-50; Lucy L. Wenhold, "The First Fort of San Marcos de Apalachee," F.H.Q., XXXIV (April, 1954), pp. 301-313.

clear he had no desire to get in a dispute with the Father Provincial or the friars, as he only wanted to take the necessary measures to insure peace in the provinces. He hastened to add that Spain's enemies, especially the English, might establish themselves in Florida if the Spaniards relaxed their vigilance. It was essential to maintain the Apalachee garrison at an effective level of strength. Also, it was imperative that the St. Marks port be observed closely and that a presidio be constructed there as quickly as possible.[23]

Governor Rebolledo selected an incident which occurred in Guale to drive home to the Franciscans the need for soldiers in the provinces. He reminded the friars when the Reverend Father Difinidor Sebastían Martínez returned from Guale with disturbing news of an English intrusion into the Georgia country that the Father Provincial became quite excited and asked him whether he intended to send additional infantrymen to Guale to protect the missionaries. The governor assured Father Provincial

---

[23] [Governor Rebolledo's] Notificacíon y Repuesta [to the Franciscans], August 5, 1657, Stet. Coll. Escrib. de Cam., Leg. 155, pp. 40-50.

San Antonio that his primary responsibility as the governor was to protect the provinces and its inhabitants
against enemy incursions. He was aware of the threat
which an enemy intrusion posed to religious work and to
Spain's suzerainty in Florida.[24] Apparently, however,
the friars wanted soldiers only when an invasion was emi-
nent.

Governor Rebolledo expressed his firm conviction
that the Franciscans had a responsibility to encourage the
Indians in their doctrinas to like rather than dislike the
soldiers. And, until the Crown declared its intention on
the military situation in Apalachee, the policies he had
established were not to be regarded as final. Rebolledo
did not intend to increase the garrison strength again
until he received word from the Crown. He decided to
postpone, for the time, construction of the fort at St.
Marks. The governor noted that he had made these decisions in an attempt to re-establish good relations with
the Franciscans in the province. As an additional proof
of his apparently good intentions, Governor Rebolledo

---

[24]Ibid.

indicated the possibility of reducing the garrison
strength from twelve to eight soldiers as a temporary
measure. The governor, in the event that he did not reduce the garrison, anticipated no difficulty in the soldier's procurement of food, for Apalachee, contrary to
Franciscan indications, enjoyed a good harvest. In addition, the Indians had received payment already for a
quantity of food sufficient to feed a twelve man garrison.[25] There is no evidence that he actually reduced the
garrison force.

Governor Rebolledo expressed his earnest hope that
the Franciscans would cooperate with the soldiers rather
than work at cross-purposes, for the conduct of some of
the friars had been deplorable. The Franciscans who tried
to turn the Indians against the military deserved to be
punished. Rebolledo acknowledged his desire to cooperate
with all of the friars, but made his intent clear not to
stand by and watch the Franciscans undermine his efforts
to secure Apalachee province militarily. He assured the
Father Provincial that any individual who mistreated the

---

[25] Ibid.

Indians was to be punished regardless of that person's
stature in the government or the church. This concluded
Governor Rebolledo's lengthy answer to the Franciscan pe-
tition of August 4, 1657. August 6, the scribe, Juan
Moreno y Segovia, went to the Franciscan convent in St.
Augustine where he read Governor Rebolledo's reply to the
Fathers.[26]

After Governor Rebolledo finished his reply to the
Franciscans, he prepared a set of instructions to guide
Lieutenant Antonio de Sertucha in the administration of
Apalachee. First, Rebolledo ordered him to take extensive
efforts to insure that the Indians were treated well so
they would not become restless. Whoever employed the
Indians was to remunerate them for their services. Also
the Apalachees were to receive payment for any food which
they provided the garrison, and they would not have to
supply food to the Spanish military or civilians--even
for pay--unless they chose to do so. The provincial
lieutenant, in the future, was not to permit a Franciscan
to interfere in any matter which fell under royal

---

[26]Ibid.

jurisdiction, such as administering punishment to an
Indian. It mattered not whether the Indian was guilty of
the most grievous offense against the church or Crown.
If a situation arose which required that an Indian should
receive punishment, the Franciscan might administer it
after satisfying certain requirements. First, the friar
was to inform the military authorities fully about the
nature of the Indian's misconduct. After the friar stated
his case, the authorities were to stipulate whether or not
the situation demanded a type of punishment as a cor-
rective. Then, and only then, was a friar to mete out
punishment to an Indian. Rebolledo included one exception
to the rule. If some of the friar's older neophytes became lax in fulfilling their religious obligations, the
rule would not apply, and the Fathers had the right to
take disciplinary action against the adults. Governor
Rebolledo instructed the provincial lieutenant to assist
the Franciscans as much as he could in their religious
efforts. The lieutenant, in particular, was to see that
the Indians obeyed the religious instructions which the
Fathers gave them. Province lieutenants, henceforth, were
not to permit anyone to punish a cacique or principal man,

irrespective of the act which the Indian had committed.

When a tribal leader committed an offense, the province

commander was to take him into custody and transfer the

individual to St. Augustine where the governor was to de-

cide the case.[27]

Included in the instructions to Lieutenant Sertucha

was an ordinance which pertained to the port at St. Marks.

When a vessel came to St. Marks, the lieutenant was to in-

quire immediately to ascertain the embarkation point of

the craft and also the purpose which brought the ship to

Apalachee. This information was to be forwarded to the

governor at St. Augustine as speedily as possible. The

governor would then dispatch a courier to Apalachee with

instructions. During the interim, the lieutenant was not

to allow the ship to sail from the Apalachee port, but he

was to furnish the crew with food if necessary. The lieu-

tenant was to refuse permission to the captain of any ves-

sel to take more food than necessary to feed the crew.

Any food surplus in the province was to go into a reserve

---

[27]Instrucíon [from Governor Rebolledo for Apala-
chee], August 8, 1657, Stet. Coll. Escrib. de Cam., Leg.
155, pp. 56-58.

to remedy deficiencies at St. Augustine which occurred all too frequently. Governor Rebolledo stated his intentions to send ships each year to Apalachee to transport provisions back to the presidio. The ships were to carry to the friars whatever supplies their Superiors in the Order at Havana wished to send them. If a ship came to St. Marks, after the needs of St. Augustine had been satisfied, then the lieutenant was to permit the craft to take on a cargo. The Indians knew enough to evaluate the worth of their produce as they had sold goods oftentimes in the past to visiting ships. The ordinances were not intended to prohibit the Indians from conducting trade, but were intended to regulate it in the interest of themselves and of the Crown. Any items which the Franciscans in Apalachee wished to send to their Superiors in Havana were to be delivered on the ship's return voyage to St. Augustine. Finally, the lieutenant was to inform the governor if the friars tried to impede the execution of the instructions, in which case the necessary measures could be taken to put an end to their obstructionist tactics.[28]

---

[28] Ibid.

On August 11, 1657, Governor Diego de Rebolledo
sent a strongly-worded statement to the Father Provincial
in St. Augustine criticizing Franciscan activities in
Apalachee. The governor asserted the Father Provincial
had done his share also to create disorder in the province. Rebolledo charged that he advised not to send
Friar Alonso del Moral and Friar Miguel Garcon to Apalachee, for the province had no shortage of priests. In
addition, Father Moral and Father Garcon did not know the
language of the Apalachees, and they had little experience in mission work. Governor Rebolledo affirmed that
he made the Father Provincial aware of the need for friars
in Timucua. Regretfully, the Father Provincial did not
send the friars where they were needed--rather he ordered
them to go to Apalachee. Moral and Garcon were not long
in the province before they began to create problems for
his administration. Soon after their arrival, the reports
were received from Sergeant-Major Adrian de Cañicares
which indicated that Father Moral and Father Garcon sought
to get the other Franciscans of the province to help them
get the soldiers withdrawn. Moral and Garcon had worked
among the Indians in a diligent effort to turn them

against the soldiers and to get them to request their removal. Rebolledo pointed out to the Father Provincial
that the priests distorted the picture completely and mis-
represented the facts. Adjutant Pedro de la Puerta had
made an investigation in July to ascertain whether or not
the Indians were mistreated as Moral and Garcon indicated.[29]

Adjutant Puerta carried out his orders faithfully,
and he found no evidence that the garrison soldiers mistreated the Apalachees. No spirit of restlessness existed among the Indians. Sergeant-Major Cañicares lent
additional substance to the Adjutant's findings as he had
discovered no uneasiness. Both officers indicated the
Apalachees had reflected a remarkable degree of calmness,
when one considered that the Franciscans had done so much
to excite them. The soldiers did nothing to stir up the
Indians, but the Franciscans, particularly Moral and
Garcon, had endeavored to make them restless. Because
their conduct tended to disturb the Indians, the governor

---

[29] Exortacíon y Requerimiento, August 11, 1657,
Stet. Coll. Escrib. de Cam., Leg. 155, pp. 59-61.

concluded that the Father Provincial had no proper course of action but to reassign them to another province.[30]

Juan Moreno y Segovia, the royal scribe, read Governor Rebolledo's message to the Father Provincial. Father San Antonio listened to the verbal communique, and asked the scribe to give him a copy of it for his files which apparently he did not do. The Father Provincial also made reference to the August 4 petition which the Franciscans sent to Governor Rebolledo in which they asked him to remove the troops from Apalachee and not to proceed with his plans to construct a fort at St. Marks. Father San Antonio observed regretfully that the governor had not supplied him with a written reply to the petition, for he wished to have Rebolledo's replies in writing.[31] Juan Moreno y Segovia carried the Father Provincial's

---

[30]Ibid. See also Sergeant-Major Adrian de Cañicares to Governor Rebolledo, May 8, 1657, Stet. Coll. Escrib. de Cam., Leg. 155, pp. 51-52; Same to Same, May 21, 1657, Stet. Coll. Escrib. de Cam., Leg. 155, pp. 52-53; Same to Same, July 18, 1657, Stet. Coll. Escrib. de Cam., Leg. 155, p. 55; Adjutant Pedro la Puerta to Governor Rebolledo, July 12, 1657, Stet. Coll. Escrib. de Cam., Leg. 155, p. 54.

[31]Peticíon [of the Father Provincial and the Franciscans to Governor Rebolledo], August 11, 1657, Stet. Coll. Escrib. de Cam., Leg. 155, p. 62.

petition to the governor. Rebolledo indicated that he had
reached the end of his patience with the Franciscans, and
intended to present his facts to the Crown to decide the
matter.[32]

The royal scribe went to the Franciscan friary
August 18, 1657, where he read Governor Rebolledo's reply
to the padres. When Juan Moreno y Segovia finished, the
Father Provincial handed him a petition to deliver to the
governor. The Father Provincial acknowledged that he had
received Rebolledo's request to reassign Father Moral and
Father Garcon. Father San Antonio noted that Governor
Rebolledo had used as a reason for his request the impli-
cation that the friars intrigued with the Indians in an
effort to turn them against the soldiers. Rebolledo had
singled out Father Moral and Father Garcon as the principal culprits in Apalachee. The Father Provincial regretted that the governor had regarded the priests' conduct as analogous to that of criminals, and had stated
that they deserved to be punished to provide an example

---

[32]Repuesta [of Governor Rebolledo to the Franciscan
Petición], August 17, 1657, Stet. Coll. Escrib. de Cam.,
Leg. 155, pp. 62-63.

for the other Franciscans in Apalachee. The Provincial indicated that Governor Rebolledo provided him with no firm evidence to substantiate his accusations against the friars. Since no evidence was produced other than the reports of the military in the province, Father San Antonio reaffirmed his intention to keep the friars in Apalachee until the charges against them were proved.[33]

The scribe delivered the Father Provincial's reply to Governor Rebolledo. Rebolledo asserted that there were sufficient reasons why Father Moral and Father Garcon should not be allowed to remain in Apalachee. The whole controversy had resulted in nothing but confusion and an unpleasant state of affairs. Whereas the governor had attempted to keep the province quiet and calm by trying to keep disruptive influences out of the area, the Father Provincial had skirted consistently the issue and had not acted in the best interest of the church or Crown by his persistent desire to keep Moral and Garcon in Apalachee. The governor admitted the controversy which had developed could not be resolved in Florida, and he intended to send

---

[33] Peticíon [of the Father Provincial San Antonio], n.d., Stet. Coll. Escrib. de Cam., Leg. 155, pp. 63-64.

his case to the Council of the Indies which would decide
it. The Franciscans could carry their argument wherever
they desired. Governor Rebolledo forwarded the visita
documents and the papers which related to it to the
Council of the Indies. The principal cause of the 1656
rebellion, he concluded, was the fact that the Franciscans
stirred up the Indians. To prove his point, Rebolledo
could point to a number of documents wherein the Indians
had testified about priestly misconduct.[34]

The Sons of St. Francis were not inactive either in
their effort to show that they had not caused the uprising. It had resulted because of Governor Rebolledo's
heavy-handed policies. The soldiers had forced the Indians to carry heavy cargoes from Apalachee to St. Augustine,
a distance of more than one hundred leagues. Because of
the hardship imposed on the Indians, many of them had died
on the way to St. Augustine. Such administrative policies
did nothing more than undermine years of arduous labor in
the mission fields. Rebolledo, the friars admitted, had

---

[34] Repuesta [of Governor Rebolledo to the Fran-
ciscans], August 19, 1657, Stet. Coll. Escrib. de Cam.,
Leg. 155, pp. 65-66.

not inaugurated the custom of using the Indians as port-

ers. During the administration of his predecessor, two

hundred Indians were required to carry burdens to St.

Augustine and not even ten of them ever returned to their

homes. One Franciscan, Father Gomez, maintained that the

soldiers had treated the Indians like slaves. The Indians

resented having to carry cargoes of corn on their backs

like pack animals. This virtual enslavement had caused

the Indians to rise up in rebellion. Religious work had

progressed in Apalachee and Timucua before the rebellion

occurred. The uprising, the friar observed, was put down

with unwarranted severity. There was no compelling reason

to execute eleven of the caciques. The Franciscans

brought these facts to the attention of the Council of

the Indies and the Crown so that remedial action could be

taken.[35]

The visita papers and the Franciscan reports

reached the Council of the Indies, and the administrative

---

[35]Letter from Friar Juan Gomez, March 13, 1657,
Archivo General de Indias 54-5-10, Document 73 (hereinafter cited as A.G.I.); Fray Juan Gomez to Father Francisco Martínez, Comisario de la Provincia de Florida,
April 4, 1657, A.G.I., 54-5-10, Document 74.

body took the matter under consideration. There was an
unsigned letter which protested the way Governor Rebolledo
treated the soldiers in the presidio at St. Augustine.
The Council of the Indies studied the evidence against
Rebolledo as well as the documents which he submitted to
defend himself. In July, 1657, the Council members recommended to the Crown that Diego de Rebolledo be removed
from the governorship and that his residencia be taken.
The governor died before Crown officials had the opportunity to conduct his residencia and to press charges
against him in the event that the evidence warranted an
indictment.[36]

---

[36] Council of the Indies to the Crown, June 15,
1657, A.G.I. 53-1-6, Document 68; Council of the Indies
to the Crown, July 1, 1657, A.G.I. 54-5-10, Document 75;
Council of the Indies to the Crown, July 7, 1657, A.G.I.
53-1-6, Document 70. The residencia was an inquiry which
all Crown officials faced at the close of their term of
office. If the official was found guilty of malfeasance
of duty, he was fined or imprisoned or both. If he were
exonerated, he often obtained a promotion to a better
post.

CHAPTER V

SPAIN'S REACTION TO THE ENGLISH

INTRUSION IN THE CAROLINAS

At the middle of the seventeenth century, Spanish-
Indian relations in Florida appeared well-ordered.  Franciscan friars worked among the Indians in Guale, Timucua,
and Apalachee, and the mission list of 1655 reflects the
success of the missionaries.  There existed, according to
the Franciscan reports, thirty-eight missions which minis-
tered to the spiritual needs of several thousand neophytes.
Seventy friars served in Florida at the time, most of whom
worked away from St. Augustine and among the Indians.  The
mission system extended from St. Augustine northward to
the Port Royal area and westward to the Gulf of Mexico.
Although the Franciscan friars labored primarily in the
doctrinos (religious districts) of Guale, Apalachee, and
Timucua, they did make occasional trips into south Florida
and into the hinterland of the Georgia country.  Disease,
inclement weather, inadequate supplies, Indian rebellions,

and opposition on the part of governors such as Diego de Rebolledo hindered considerably the work of the Fathers. In spite of these obstacles, however, the Franciscans achieved much. They erected no enormous and enduring temporal structures as evidence of their work. On the contrary, the priests had simple buildings made of the flimsiest material, which they used as chapels. Oftentimes they did not have the items necessary to use in offering the sacraments. The chapels frequently lacked ornaments which were essential to carry on the work of the faith. Yet, the friars devoted themselves to the work in Florida with an unusual degree of personal detachment.

The friars, irrespective of their devotion, encountered difficulties which would have discouraged all but the hardiest of individuals. Discipline of the Indian presented a problem which never ceased to bother the friars. Because the Indians' rather haphazard agricultural technology quickly exhausted the soil's fertility, they often were forced to move their villages. When the food resources dwindled to the danger point, the Indian temporarily forsook his hoe and ax and fled to the woods

in search of food. There he gathered in season, grapes,
berries, roots, and nuts, and the friar followed him into
the wilderness in a desperate effort to maintain the faith
among his charges. Another type of discipline problem
developed when the Indians revolted against Spanish authority, such as occurred in Timucua in 1656. The Franciscans, as a rule, preferred to work in the absence of
soldiers, for they maintained that the military created
unnecessary problems with the Indians. A basic cause of
the conflict between the friar and the soldier was over
the end toward which they labored. The friar concerned
himself with the Indian's spiritual needs, and he worked
best in an atmosphere of peace. On the other hand, the
soldier was stationed in the province to preserve the
peace against intrusions by European powers and heathen
Indians. Florida governors decided after 1656, over
vigorous and sustained Franciscan protests, to keep troops
in force in all three of the Florida provinces.[1]

Apalachee, prior to 1656, did not have a garrison

---

[1]Lanning, The Spanish Missions of Georgia, pp. 164-
190, 191-200; Bolton and Ross, The Debatable Land, pp. 28-
44; Gannon, The Cross in the Sand, pp. 49-67.

as such. What she did have was an observation force which usually consisted of no more than three men. The Timucuan rebellion, however, changed this situation and Governor Rebolledo increased the size of the garrison to twelve, making it thereby a defensive force. The Franciscans protested to the Crown the governor's decision to station additional troops in Apalachee. The Council of the Indies, however, took no action to reduce the garrison. In fact, the garrison size was increased until by 1662 there exixted in the province forty soldiers. The fort which Rebolledo projected at St. Marks was not constructed until 1680 during Governor Pablo Hita Salazar's administration.[2]

Spanish Florida approached a new era in 1657. Before a decade passed, St. Augustine faced a serious English

---

[2] [Governor Rebolledo's] Notificacíon y Repuesta [to the Franciscans], August 5, 1657, Stet. Coll. Escrib. de Cam., Leg. 155, pp. 40-50; Rebolledo to the King, October 18, 1657, Brooks, The Unwritten History of Old St. Augustine, pp. 102-105; Council of the Indies to the Crown, June 15, 1657, A.G.I., 53-1-6, Document 68; Same to Same, July 1, 1657, A.G.I., 54-5-10, Document 75; Same to Same, July 7, 1657, A.G.I., 53-1-6, Document 70. All are in the John B. Stetson Collection. Governor Aranjuiz y Cotes to the Crown, August 8, 1662, A.G.I., 58-2-2, Document 8, Stet. Coll.; Wenhold, "The First Fort of San Marcos de Apalachee," F.H.Q., XXXIV (April, 1954), 301-313.

threat which originated out of Carolina bases. While England did not actually establish a settlement until 1670, several English expeditions made appearances in the Carolinas during the 1660's in an effort to explore out the land and to use the knowledge gained therefrom to attract settlers from British Colonies in the Caribbean and elsewhere. These British expeditions came at a time when the increasing slave economy of Caribbean islands such as Barbados was forcing many small landholders out of agriculture. The technological unemployment which resulted influenced many of these individuals to seek homes in the Carolinas, especially South Carolina. Since Spain maintained no garrison north of the Savannah River after 1657, there was nothing to prohibit English intrusions in the area.[3]

England made no concentrated effort to colonize the Carolinas prior to 1660. The land itself was granted as early as 1629 with the desire that it would be settled, but such was not the case. King Charles I bestowed on Sir Robert Heath in 1629 a grant of land which extended "from

[3]The expeditions referred to were led by William Hilton and Robert Sandford.

the Ocean of the east and the west as far as the Continent
extends and all islands within the degrees of 31 + 36
Northern latitude."[4] This land grant reflected a considerable magnanimity on the part of His Majesty, for it
included not only the Carolinas but most of the Georgia
country. As such it encroached very definitely within
that sphere of influence where Spain physically occupied
the terrain through missions and presidios. Robert Heath,
however, failed to develop the enormous tract the King
gave him, so in 1663, King Charles II awarded the Carolinas to eight Englishmen collectively known as the Lords
Proprietors. On this occasion, the English crown reflected an even more magnanimous spirit, for Charles established the southern boundary of the grant at 29 degrees
north. Since the grant ran from the Atlantic to the
Pacific, it included Santa Fé and El Paso within its
jurisdiction.[5]

---

[4]Sir Robert Heath's Patent 5 Charles 1st (30 Oct:
1629) in Collections of the South Carolina Historical
Society, V (Richmond: William Ellis Jones, Book and Job
Printer, 1897), 3, hereinafter cited as Collections
S.C.H.S.

[5]Alexander Samuel Salley, Jr. (ed.), Narratives of
Early Carolina 1650-1708, Original Narratives (New York:

Some time elapsed before actual colonization took place in the Carolinas. In the interim English voyages of exploration took place along the coast in an effort to gather data on the flora, fauna, water, and land resources of the area. Captain William Hilton, who lived on Barbados, sailed to the Carolinas in 1663 and explored the area around Cape Fear. Impressed with what he saw while there, Captain Hilton gave a good report on the area when he returned to Barbados. Hardly had he returned when the Barbadians asked him to go again to the Carolinas to survey the physical resources of the region, for the Barbadians hoped to use Hilton's report to counteract unfavorable verdicts which a group of New Englanders circulated about the Carolinas. The New Englanders, who settled in the Cape Fear region, quickly became disgruntled. There was no adequate port, and the soil and weather conditions did not measure up to their expectations. Consequently, the New Englanders decided to go elsewhere, but they

---

Charles Scribner's Sons, 1911), p. 33, hereinafter cited as Narratives of Early Carolina. The eight proprietors were: Earl of Clarendon, Duke of Albemarle, Lord Craven, Lord Berkeley, Lord Ashley (afterwards Earl of Shaftesbury), Sir George Carteret, Sir William Berkeley, and Sir John Colleton.

verbally castigated the Carolinas, and the Lords Proprietors felt constrained to take measures to mitigate their
indictment of the area.[6]

Captain Hilton yielded to the Barbadians request
and prepared to return to the Carolinas. This time, however, he determined to cruise the coastline south of Cape
Fear to point out the benefits, if any, which existed
there. On August 23, 1663, Hilton appeared off the Carolina Coast not far to the north of Santa Elena. Moving
down the coast, the commander entered the harbor at Santa
Elena and encountered a river which he referred to as the
Jordan.[7] The Captain was not long in the bay before the
Edisto Indians of the area made their presence known. The
Edisto's climbed aboard Hilton's vessel and quickly demon-
strated to him a knowledge of the Spanish language and an

---

[6]William Hilton, A True Relation of a Voyage upon
discovery of part of the Coast of Florida, from the Lat.
of 31 Deg. to 33 Deg. 45m. North Lat., in the ship ad-
venture, William Hilton Commander, and Commissioner with
Captain Anthony Long and Peter Fabian set forth by several
Gentlemen and Merchants of the Island of Barbadoes; sailed
from Spikes Bay Aug. 10, 1663, Collections S.C.H.S., V,
18, hereinafter cited as Hilton's Relation.

[7]Hilton's Relation, p. 19. See especially note 1.

acquaintance with firearms. The Indians informed the
Englishman that Franciscan missionaries served in the
area, and indicated that Spanish soldiers visited the region from time to time. St. Augustine, they noted, was
but ten days distance by foot. Spaniards, who used the
intercoastal waterway, cut the time in half. The Indians
also pointed out to Hilton that they retained in their
villages some of his countrymen who had been shipwrecked
on the coast just prior to his arrival. Captain Hilton,
who feared for the safety of the English sailors, undertook to retrieve them from the Indians. In order to expedite the matter, he seized several of the Edistos and
held them as hostages in an effort to force the natives
to hand over his countrymen. While engaged in his at-
tempts to rescue the sailors, Captain Hilton carried on
a lively correspondence with the English castaways and a
party of Spanish soldiers who had come from St. Augustine
to investigate the incident.[8]

The Indians turned over to Captain Hilton some of
the captives they held shortly after he had seized the

---

[8]Ibid., pp. 19-25.

Edisto hostages. One of the English sailors, whose name
is not mentioned, informed Captain Hilton about the presence of Spanish soldiers in the Santa Elena area. Hilton
quickly concluded that the Spaniards had come up the coast
for no other purpose than to take the English to St.
Augustine for interrogation, so on September 21, he wrote
a letter to the captives to inform them that he intended
to secure their rescue by whichever means the situation
demanded. Hilton assured those still in captivity that
he had already rescued some of their party, and that he
anticipated liberating them soon. He encouraged the
prisoners if they had the opportunity to forward any
information which they had on the Spanish soldiers and
their intentions. Captain Hilton gave the letter to the
Indians who carried it to the English captives.[9]

September 22, Captain Alonso de Arguelles, who com-
manded the Spanish expedition which had come to Santa
Elena in search of the castaways, wrote Captain Hilton.
Captain Arguelles informed him that the Spanish

---

[9] Hilton to the English Prisoners, September 21,
1663, Hilton's Relation, Collections S.C.H.S., V, 26.

authorities at St. Augustine had received word of a shipwreck in the Santa Elena area and that Governor Alonso
Aranjuez y Cotes ordered him up the coast to render assistance, if necessary, to the stranded mariners. The
Spanish captain advised the English captain to pay a ran-
som, if necessary, to get his countrymen out of the hands
of the Edisto Indians. Neither Hilton nor any of his crew
understood Spanish and failed to understand the reason
which brought Captain Arguelles to Santa Elena. Consequently, Hilton wrote Arguelles, September 23, that he was
unable to understand his letter. Captain Hilton informed
Arguelles that he had made an attempt to liberate his
countrymen by detaining Indian prisoners aboard his ship
whom he intended to retain there until the Indians released the sailors.[10]

On September 24, Captain Hilton wrote again to the
English seamen at Santa Elena. He informed them that he
had received their reply which Captain Arguelles gra-
ciously consented to include in his communique to Hilton.

---

[10]Arguelles to Hilton, September 22, 1663, Hilton's
Relation, pp. 25-26; Hilton to Arguelles, September 23,
1663, Hilton's Relation, p. 27. All are in Collections
S.C.H.S., V.

Captain Hilton expressed his concern over the fact that no
exchange of prisoners was yet arranged and asked William
Davis, the person to whom he addressed his remarks, to inform the Edistos that he intended to sail away with the
Indian captives he had aboard unless they released the remaining English prisoners.  In addition, Captain Hilton
directed Davis to thank Captain Arguelles, when he saw
him, for a gift of pork and venison.[11]

Later that day, Hilton wrote to Captain Arguelles,
and informed the Spanish commandant that he had had enough
of the Indian's procrastination.  Either the Edistos were
to release the Englishmen, or he was going to depart from
the area with the captive Indians.  Hilton concluded his
letter on a conciliatory note by thanking the Spaniard for
the gift of food.  Meanwhile, Captain Arguelles wrote to
Hilton to inform him that the Edistos feared the English
had the idea in mind of harming them.  The Spanish captain
urged Captain Hilton to adopt a more conciliatory attitude
toward the Indians.  Arguelles insinuated that the Edistos

---

[11]Hilton to the English Prisoners, September 24,
1663, Hilton's Relation, Collections S.C.H.S., V, 27.

intended no harm to the English sailors, and he encouraged the English commander to give the Indians some spades, axes, knives, and beads as a token of his appreciation for their rescuing the sailors. At this point the correspondence between Hilton and Arguelles stopped, and there is no clear indication that Hilton managed to retrieve the remaining prisoners in the hands of the Indians.[12]

Although Captain Hilton went to great efforts to rescue the stranded mariners, the primary purpose of his trip was to survey the physical resources of the area which he proceeded to do. He noted that Santa Elena had a large and deep harbor which would accommodate easily a good deal of commerce. Hilton found that in most places the soil was very fertile. Oftentimes, the top soil extended for at least a foot in depth. As a result, the Indians were able to grow all kinds of scope such as corn, melons, squash, beans, and yams. From the forest, the Indians gathered nuts, berries, and fruits such as the grape and persimmon to supplement their diet. Since trees

---

[12] Hilton to Arguelles, September 24, 1663, Hilton's Relations, Collections S.C.H.S., V, 27-28; Arguelles to Hilton, September 23, 1663, Hilton's Relations, Collections S.C.H.S., V, 28.

grew profusely, the Carolinas abounded with deer, turkey, squirrels, and quail, but venison constituted the principal source of meat for the Indians. The lakes, streams, and bays teemed with aquatic creatures. Bass, bream, sturgeon, catfish, carp, and mussels were found in great quantities in fresh water. Clams, oysters, shrimp, and a multitude of fish were harvested regularly from salt water. Ducks, geese, marsh hens, and snipes inhabited the marshy areas of both salt and fresh water. Hilton's report as such flowed with praise of the Carolinas, and it served as an excellent type of promotional literature with which to attract potential colonizers.[13]

In 1664 the Barbadians succeeded in establishing a settlement on the Cape Fear River in present-day North Carolina. The Lords Proprietors appointed John Yeamans to serve as governor of the new colony which was called Clarendon County. Robert Sandford was selected by the Proprietors to serve as the secretary of the colony. The infant settlement, however, did not thrive as anticipated and most of the settlers became disgruntled. Early in

---

[13] Hilton's Relation, Collections S.C.H.S., V, 22-24.

1666, Governor Yeamans, in an effort to find a better site

for his colony, instructed Secretary Robert Sandford to

conduct explorations to the south of the Cape Fear region,

which he did. Sandford searched the coast thoroughly, and

concurred with the favorable verdict which Hilton had

given about the richness of the soil and the abundance of

wild life that existed throughout the area. More impor-

tant than these observations, however, was the fact that

he carried an important figure, Doctor Henry Woodward, on

this voyage. Doctor Woodward indicated to Sandford before

they made landfall that he wanted to remain among the

Indians if it was at all feasible in order to become ac-

quainted with the geographical features of the land and to

learn the Indian languages of the area. Sandford dis-

cussed the matter with the Edisto cacique who expressed

his pleasure with Woodward's intentions to live among the

Indians.[14] Sandford had no fear for Doctor Woodward's

safety because

---

[14]Robert Sandford, A Relation of a Voyage on the
Coast of the Province of Carolina, Formerly called Florida,
in the Continent of the Northern American, from Charles
River near Cape Feare, in the County of Clarendon, and the
Lat. of 34 Deg: to Port Royall, in the North Lat. of 32

The Cassique placed Woodward by him upon the Throne,
and after lead him forth and shewed him a large
field of Maiz which hee told him should bee his,
then hee brought him the Sister of the Indian that
I had with mee telling nim that shee should tend
him and dresse his victualls and be careful amongst
us. I stayed a while being wounderous civilly
treated after their manner, and giveing Woodward
formall possession of the whole Country to hold as
Tennant att Will of the Right Honoble the Lords
Proprietors, I retorned aboard and immediately
weighed and fell downe.[15]

Although Sandford did not feel that Woodward was in any

kind of danger, he took the Edisto cacique's nephew with

him when he departed from the area.

Henry Woodward wasted no time once Sandford weighed

anchor. He set about immediately to learn as much as he

could about the countryside, and undertook to learn the

Indian languages. Spanish infantrymen captured Woodward

soon afterwards and carried him to St. Augustine. Doctor

Woodward ingratiated himself with the Spanish people once

he reached the capital city, for he became a convert to

---

Deg: begun 14th June, 1666; Performed by Robert Sandford
Essquire, Secretary and Chiefe Register for the Lords Proprietors of their County of Clarendon, in the Province
aforesaid, Narratives of Early Carolina, p. 105, hereinafter cited as Sandford's Relation.

[15]Sandford's Relation, Narratives of Early Carolina, p. 105.

Catholicism and served as the garrison's physician. As a
result, Woodward had practically as much freedom in St.
Augustine as he desired. This stay among the Spaniards
gave him the opportunity to evaluate the relative strength
and weakness of the Spanish defensive machinery in Florida.
He continued also to study the Indian tongues, which later
on made him very useful to the Carolina settlers as an
interpreter and diplomat. Woodward stayed at St. Augustine until the English pirate, Robert Searles rescued him
in 1668. Searles, who maintained his principal base of
operations in the Caribbean, employed a clever bit of
stratagem when he launched his raid against the Spanish
city. The pirate captured some Spanish vessels and forced
the captive crews to sail the ships into the St. Augustine
harbor while he and his fellow bandits remained below. As
a result the pirates took the city completely by surprise
and sacked it with virtually no opposition. Searles
gathered all of the city's valuables and took Doctor
Woodward with him to serve as the ship's surgeon when he
sailed away. In the long run, Searles' raid proved beneficial to St. Augustine for the Spanish Crown then appro-
priated funds to construct a stone fort at the capital--

one that Pedro Menéndez de Avilés had recommended a hundred years earlier.[16]

In 1669, Joseph West and a group of Barbadian colonizers, Henry Woodward among them, departed for the Carolinas to establish a settlement. They made landfall on the Ashley River at Albemarle Point in 1670 and called their settlement Charles Town. Although Barbados contributed the original impetus of settlers to the Carolina colony, Jamaica and the mainland colony, Virginia, sent a sizeable number of settlers soon afterwards. Various reasons contributed to the increment of the colonists. Certainly the promotional literature of William Hilton and Robert Sandford influenced a large number of disillusioned Caribbean farmers in their decision to migrate to the Carolinas. The fact that small tobacco farmers had to compete with large sugar planters with slave labor

---

[16]Bolton and Ross, The Debatable Land, p. 31; Joseph Dalton to Lord Ashley, Collections S.C.H.S., V, 193. See also Collections S.C.H.S., V, 188, footnote 1, 190, footnote 1, and 191, footnote 2. Don Francisco de la Guerra y de la Vega to the Viceroy of New Spain, July 7, 1668, A.G.I., 58-2-2; Albert C. Manucy (ed. and trans.), The History of Castillo de San Marcos and Fort Matanzas (Washington: United States Government Printing Office, Reprint 1955), pp. 12-13.

caused an even larger number of people to seek homes elsewhere.[17]

The Treaty of Madrid, concluded by England and
Spain in 1670, confirmed the English claim to the Carolinas. England was to have no rights south of the Savannah River. The treaty, to be exact, confirmed possession
rights only over property actually occupied, and the area
between the Savannah and Altamaha Rivers came to be known
as a "No Man's Land" over which neither England nor Spain
exerted much influence, although Spain rightly asserted a
vigorous claim to it. The Madrid Treaty was signed but
the Carolinians paid little attention to the terms once
they learned of the features which tended to circumscribe
their expansion activities. Doctor Woodward, soon after
reaching Albemarle Point in 1670, journeyed to the Indian
village Cufitachiqui where Hernando de Soto had visited
one hundred and thirty years earlier. The interior of
the Carolina country vividly impressed Woodward, and he
quickly realized the fur trade potential of the region.

---

[17] Edward McCrady, The History of South Carolina
under the Proprietory Government 1670-1719, I (New York:
The Macmillan Company, 1897), p. 129.

He recognized also the necessity of maintaining friendship with the Indians while the English colony was relatively weak, so he concluded a treaty of friendship. This was the beginning of his diplomatic efforts, which in coming years made the Carolinas a thriving colony.[18]

The authorities at St. Augustine and Charles Town experienced anxious moments very soon after the English colony was established. A ship from Barbados bound for Charles Town put in at the Spanish held St. Catherine Island in Guale to acquire wood and water. A fight broke out between the ship's crew and the Spanish garrison stationed there, and a number of the Englishmen were taken as prisoners. As soon as Governor Sayle, at Charles Town, heard of the affair, he sent a delegation to the island to demand the release of his countrymen. Two members of the delegation, Joseph Bailey and John Collins, handed Governor Sayle's demand to the Spanish commandant. Instead of acceding to the English request, the Spaniards arrested

---

[18] Francis Gardiner Davenport (ed.), European Treaties Bearing on the History of the United States and Its Dependencies, II (Washington: Carnegie Institution, 1929), p. 194; H. Woodward to Sir John Yeaman, September 10, 1670, Collections S.C.H.S., V, 186-188.

Bailey and Collins and delivered them to Governor Francisco de la Guerra y de la Vega (1664-1671) at St. Augustine.  There, they stayed for at least two years, for Bailey wrote a letter in 1672 protesting the fact that not much had been done to get him out of the clutches of his Spanish captors.[19]

During the two year interval, the Spaniards took more direct means with which to deal with the English at Charles Town whom they considered as a serious threat. Governor Guerra, apparently unaware of the Madrid Treaty, decided in the latter part of 1670 to send an expedition to eradicate the English colony before it became too strong.  Accordingly, he ordered Juan Menéndez Marqúes to lead an expedition of soldiers and Indian allies against Charles Town and destroy it.  The Edisto Indians warned the English of the approaching Spanish attack, and the Carolinians hastened to prepare whatever defenses they could in the short time which remained.  Soon afterwards,

---

[19]Mr. Mathew's Relation, Collections S.C.H.S., V, 169-171; F. O'Sullivan to Lord Ashley, Collections S.C.H.S., V, 188-190; letter from Joseph Bailey to the English Ambassador in Spain, The South Carolina Historical and Genealogical Magazine, XVIII (January, 1917), 54-56, hereinafter cited as S.C.H.G.M.

the crimson and gold waved off the entrance of Charles
Town. The Spaniards did not succeed in launching an attack against the settlement, for Providence, in the shape
of a hurricane, intervened to save the English. Governor
Guerra had dispatched the Marquéz expedition during the
hurricane season, and a tropical storm happened to move
north through the Bahama Channel at this particular time.
Shortly after Marquéz had anchored off the entrance to
the harbor, the storm struck with full force causing the
ship anchors to drag, precluding any attack against
Charles Town. Several of the ships were damaged and the
fleet limped back to St. Augustine to undergo repairs.[20]

The next few years were anxious ones for the
Spaniards at St. Augustine. The administration used
loyal Guale Indians, missionaries, and soldiers stationed
in Guale province to obtain intelligence data which they
forwarded to the Crown as quickly as it was acquired. On
March 24, 1672, Governor Manuel de Cendoya informed the

---

[20] H. Woodward to Sir John Yeamans, September 10,
1670, Collections S.C.H.S., V, 187; Don Nicolas Ponce de
León to the Queen, July 8, 1673, José Miguel Gallardo
(trans.), "The Spaniards and the English Settlement in
Charles Town," S.C.H.G.M., XXXVII (April, 1936), 57;
Crane, The Southern Frontier 1670-1732, p. 10.

Madrid government that the English possessed a fortified
city on the Ashley River.  The governor noted that already
he had asked Viceroy Mancera of New Spain and the Governor
of Havana to make troops available to him so that he could
move against Charles Town as Governor Guerra had attempted
to do two years earlier.  July 8, 1673, Sergeant-Major
Nicolas Ponce de León, who served as interim governor of
Florida while the Council of the Indies selected a replacement for Manuel de Cendoya, wrote to the Crown with
news about Carolina and Florida.  León told the Queen that
the settlement known as San Jorge or St. George was situated approximately sixty leagues north of St. Augustine.
The authorities at St. Augustine, he acknowledged, had not
tried to attack the English settlement since the Marqúez
fiasco of 1670, for the garrison lacked a sufficient number of soldiers to launch an offensive.  He also mentioned
that additional settlers had arrived at Charles Town, and
that the colony received frequently supplies from England,
Virginia, Bermuda, and Barbados.  León warned the Crown
about the possibility of an English attack on St.
Augustine and noted that if the English captured the
capital city they could cut off the extensive Spanish

shipping which came through the Bahama Channel. The
Sergeant-Major pointed out also that the Carolinians might
move against Apalachee province.[21]

From St. Marks, León observed the English could
prowl the sea lanes in the Gulf of Mexico and team up with
English Caribbean pirates to harass the galleons before
they even reached the Bahama Channel. Not only would
Spain suffer, but the poor Indians of the province would
be abandoned and the work of the church undone. Therefore, he implored the Queen to hasten the completion of
the Castillo de San Marcos, then under construction, and
to send additional reinforcements of men to the Florida
capital. The Sergeant-Major urged the Queen to send the
Windward Fleet to attack the Carolina settlement before
it gained further strength. He pointed out that this
armada, coupled with the presidio forces at St. Augustine,

---

[21]Don Manuel de Cendoya, Governor of Florida, to
the Crown, March 24, 1672, Gallardo (trans.), "The
Spaniards and the English Settlement in Charles Town,"
S.C.H.G.M., XXXVII (April, 1936), 50-51; Don Nicolas
Ponce de Leon to the Queen, July 8, 1673, Gallardo
(trans.), "The Spaniards and the English Settlement in
Charles Town," S.C.H.G.M., XXXVII (April, 1936), 57-59.

probably could remove the English menace without undue difficulty.[22]

The Spanish Crown, however, did not take any action on the Sergeant-Major's request. The English colony continued to attract new settlers, and the fur trade of the interior beckoned individuals such as Henry Woodward to risk their lives to participate in it. Although Doctor Woodward had won the allegiance of the Indians in the vicinity of Cufitachiqui in 1670, he did not succeed in gaining the friendship of the Westo Indians until 1674. This powerful tribe, which lived near the Savannah River and which guarded the approaches to the interior of the Georgia country, created fear in the minds of the other Indian groups. The fact that the Westoes had a reputation as cannibals[23] probably did nothing to diminish other Indians' respect for them. In the fall of 1674, Doctor Woodward paid a visit to the country of the Westoes.

---

[22]Don Nicolas Ponce de León to the Queen, July 8, 1673, Gallardo (trans.), "The Spaniards and the English Settlement in Charles Town," S.C.H.G.M., XXXVII (April, 1936), 57-59.

[23]Swanton, Early History of the Creek Indians, p. 166.

Having reached their villages, the Indians treated the
intrepid surgeon as if he were the principal cacique among
them. Woodward said that "haveing oyled my eyes and
joynts with beares oyl, they presented me divers deare-
skins, setting befoore me sufficient of their food to
satisfy at least half a dozen of their owne appetities."[24]
He said also that they were "well provided with arms,
amunition, tradeing cloath and other trade from the northward for which at set times of ye year they truck drest
deare skins, furrs & young Indian slaves."[25] When Woodward returned to Charles Town, some of the Westo braves
accompanied him. As evidence of his diplomatic skill with
Indians, the alliance that he formed with the Westoes was
the basic ingredient in Carolina's control over the Indians of the area until at least 1680. The Carolinians supplied the Westoes with weapons and munitions and the Indians, in turn, protected the flank of the colony from

---

[24] Henry Woodward, Discovery, A faithful relation of
my Westoe voiage begun from ye head of Ashley River the
tenth of Oct. and finished ye sixth of Nov. following,
Collections S.C.H.S., V, 459-460, hereinafter cited as
Woodward's Discovery.

[25] Ibid., p. 460.

attack by the Guale Indians south of the Savannah River who maintained allegiance to the Spanish Crown.[26]

While Woodward and his colleagues sought to shore up the defensive system of their colony, Spanish subjects to the south gave considerable attention to the question of their own preparedness. A letter of Governor Pablo de Hita y Salazar, June 15, 1675, is indicative of that interest. He went to great lengths to point out the special virtues which he felt that Apalachee province contained. With respect to the area the governor said:

> . . . in regard to the most suitable places in these Provinces for settlement by Spanish families all are agreed that the town of Apalachee [San Luis] and the surrounding territory is best because of the great fertility of the soil. If the settlers be farmers the crops will be abundant on account of the richness of the land, as may be seen by the wheat which the friars sow for their sustenance. . . . They [the settlers] will serve as a check to the enemy English and French who have settled on the bay of Mexico and are trying to advance into this territory because of the rumor of its great fertility.[27]

---

[26] Crane, The Southern Frontier 1670-1732, p. 17.

[27] Governor Pablo de Hita y Salazar to the King, June 15, 1675, Katherine Reding (trans. and ed.), "Notes and Documents--Plans for the Colonization and Defense of Apalachee, 1675," G.H.Q., IX (June, 1926), 169-170.

Governor Salazar pointed to the Canary Islands as a likely place from which to acquire individuals who would be desirable for this area. He declared to the Crown that a sizeable group of settlers, if induced to come to western Florida, would pose a serious obstacle to any advance which the English or French might contemplate in the area. Not only was the soil very fertile, but the many navigable rivers of the area such as the Suwannee, Apalachicola, Withlacoochee and others enabled goods to be moved to markets such as St. Augustine.[28]

Governor Salazar included in his report a letter addressed to the Queen in which he made an emotional appeal for Apalachee. Here he wrote that the Apalachee soil was so fertile that

> . . . by developing agriculture, such advances will be made that even the fields of Flanders will not be superior. There is so much uninhabited land that in a few years those who come, and all the present inhabitants of these provinces, will be rich from the harvests which are promised in such abundance---But their fields cannot be extended because of the inconvenience of working the land by hand; but with the introduction of oxen and plow which the settlers would use, the hard physical labor of the Indians in these crops could be

---

[28] Ibid.

avoided, and with greater knowledge the crops could be improved.[29]

The governor felt that the development of this region would go a long way toward solving the food problems of Florida, as had Governor Benito Ruíz de Salazar in the 1640's.

In the midst of strained relations between St. Augustine and Charles Town, the Florida colony received an Ecclesiastical Visitation from the Bishop of Cuba, Gabriel Díaz Vara Calderón. Basically, the Bishop came to Florida to administer the rites of Confirmation, to correct any religious abuses which might have developed, to inquire into the process of Indian conversion and to lend whatever encouragement he could to the overworked Franciscan friars. The Bishop visited Guale, Timucua, and Apalachee provinces. Bishop Calderón, who at first thought about bringing with him a team of Dominicans to assist the Franciscans in their pastoral labors, changed his mind when he feared that professional jealousy might

---

[29] Governor Pablo de Hita Salazar to the Queen, June 15, 1675, Katherine Reding (trans. and ed.), "Notes and Documents--Plans for the Colonization and Defense of Apalachee, 1675," G.H.Q., IX (June, 1926), 170-171.

develop between the two orders. Calderón traveled extensively in Florida. All together he visited thirty-seven missions, and he administered rites of Confirmation to 13,152 individuals which is indicative of how extensive and intensive the Franciscan efforts in Florida had been.[30] Whether the Indians were Christians in the Spanish sense of the word is of course subject to debate.

While traveling to the various Indian villages, Bishop Calderón made some rather interesting observations on the Florida Indians. He concluded that the women dressed too scantily to measure up to the standards of Christian decency, and he instructed them to dress more fully. He exaggerated the size of the Indian communal buhío or council house when he suggested that the house could accommodate two to three thousand individuals.[31] Regarding the physical characteristics of the Florida Indian, the Bishop wrote:

> They are fleshy, and rarely is there a small one,
> but they are weak and phlegmatic as regards work,

---

[30] Wenhold (trans.), "A 17th Century Letter of Gabriel Díaz Vara Calderón," pp. 1-14.

[31] Ibid., p. 12. This figure of course was an exaggeration.

though clever and quick to learn any art they see
done, and great carpenters as is evidenced in the
construction of their wooden churches which are
large and painstakingly wrought.[32]

Bishop Calderón's trip to Florida came at the time when

the Franciscan mission program was at its apex. After

1675, the missions declined in numbers and strength as the

Carolinians began to put pressure on Guale and Timucua

through their slave raids.

Soon after Bishop Calderón returned to Cuba the

Chisa (Yuchi) Indians,[33] who lived at the time along the

Chattahoochee River, launched a series of slave raids in

Apalachee which upset tribal tranquility and presented a

threat to the mission program. As a result, the caciques

asked the province lieutenant, Juan Fernández de Florencia,

for persmission to go against the maurauders. Florencia

readily gave his assent, and he provided the Indian arque-

busiers with ammunition. The Apalachee caciques and their

principal men quickly rounded up a substantial number of

men to go in pursuit of the Chiscas. They departed on

---

[32] Ibid.

[33] Swanton, Early History of the Creek Indians, pp.
288-289.

September 2, 1677, and headed toward the Georgia country.

After traveling for nineteen days, the Indians arrived at

the Chisca town which was heavily fortified. Anxious that

they did not betray their presence in a premature assault,

the Apalachees waited until approximately three o'clock in

the morning before they launched their attack. The rout

was complete and the Apalachees administered a sound de-

feat to the Chiscas. Lieutenant Florencia heartily

thanked the Indians for their valor, and Sergeant-Major

Leturiondo conveyed Governor Salazar's appreciation when

he visited the pueblo San Martín de Tomoli, December 22,

1677.[34]

---

[34] Juan Fernández de Florencia to Governor Pablo de Hita y Salazar, August 30, 1678, Serrano y Sanz, Documentos Historicos de la Florida y la Lusiana Siglos XVI al XVIII, pp. 207-216. See also Swanton, Early History of the Creek Indians, pp. 299-304.

CHAPTER VI

CAPTAIN ANTONIO DE ARGUELLES VISITA GENERAL

OF GUALE, DECEMBER 21, 1677

TO JANUARY 10, 1678

Guale, Timucua, and Apalachee provinces reflected
orderly Spanish-Indian relations in 1677. There existed
no visible signs of restlessness among the Indians, and
although no rebellion had occurred since 1656, Spanish
troops were stationed in all of the provinces to insure
against this possibility. The Franciscan mission system,
from all outward appearances, seemed successful. Bishop
Calderón's ecclesiastical visitation only two years
earlier seemed to confirm this. Franciscan Fathers and
Superiors alike had every reason to feel pride in their
accomplishments, for the presence of thirty-seven missions
and more than 12,000 Indian converts was sufficient evidence to justify the fact the Franciscans had succeeded.
A casual and uninformed visitor to Florida at this time
might have thought, and with some justification, that the

authorities at St. Augustine had no real reason for worry.
Yet, Governor Pablo de Hita y Salazar (1675-1680) was un-
easy.

The governor was aware of the fact that the English
controlled the coastal area north of the Savannah River
which once belonged to Spain. Although the Treaty of
Madrid (1670) supposedly curbed any aggressive intention
the Charles Town settlers had, the activities of Indian
diplomats and fur traders such as Doctor Henry Woodward
disturbed the governor. Especially disquieting was Woodward's treaty (1674) with the Westo Indians on the Savannah River who lived dangerously close to the Guale missions. This posed a threat to the Guale doctrinas. It
opened the interior of the Georgia country to the Carolina
fur merchants and exposed Timucua and Apalachee to the
possibility of an attack by land. Governor Salazar had
reason for anxiety, for the garrison at Santa Catalina
hardly seemed adequate to him to furnish protection for
Guale. Missionaries and soldiers who served in the province reported about undue tension in the province. The
data which the governor obtained indicated that the Guale
Indians reflected increasing laxness in the respect which

they showed to the representatives of the church and the
Crown. Governor Salazar was not frightened, for the Guale
Indians had not become rebellious, yet he decided to send
a representative to Guale with instructions to conduct a
general inspection of the province. Since no major inspection of any of the provinces had been held for some
time, Governor Salazar reasoned that this was the only way
to evaluate the problems which existed and take necessary
measures to ward off future difficulty.

The governor had intended to go personally to
Guale, but administrative duties weighed against this,
and he was forced to select a substitute. Governor
Salazar did not have to look far to find a competent replacement, and he chose Captain Antonio de Arguelles, a
veteran of thirty years in the Royal Service, to conduct
the investigation of Guale.[1] Satisfied with his choice,
he gave Captain Arguelles complete instructions as to the
role he was to play.

The most important part of the governor's

---

[1]Titulo de 29 de Noviembre [de 1677] por la des-
cargo, Stet. Coll. Escrib. de Cam., Leg. 156, pp. 519-522.
See also Titulo de Visitador de 6 de Noviembre de 1677,
Stet. Coll. Escrib. de Cam., Leg. 156, pp. 531-533.

instructions centered around a royal cédula which the
Crown dispatched a year earlier to all of tne imperial
officials. The king had dwelt at length on the problem
of Spanish-Indian relations in the empire possessions.
Specifically, it had come to his attention that Spaniards
mistreated the Indians throughout the Americas, and that
many governmental officials in the empire were guilty of
misconduct. These officials did not reflect at all the
confidence intrusted in and the leadership expected of
them. Not infrequently they violated their instructions
as soon as they reached their assignments. Not to be in-
convenienced by the life on the frontier, the officials
forced the Indians to give them food and shelter and to
furnish them witn beasts of burden to transport their
baggage. These same administrative officials often neg-
lected or chose not to pay the natives for their services.
These flagrant violations of royal proceaure greatly disturbed him, for he desired the Spaniards to treat the
Indians with consideration and kindness. In an effort to
solve the problem, the king put the matter before the

Council of the Indies.[2]

The Council reached a decision and the Crown ordered the Viceroys, Presidents, Judges of the Audiencia, Gobernadores, Corregidores, and other Crown officials who had contact with Indians not to require the natives to provide them with food, lodging, or beasts of burden. The cédula stipulated, however, that the Indians could furnish these items to the Spaniards if they chose to do so by their own free will. The royal officials had to pay the Indians a reasonable price for their goods. To insure that the crown officials did not feign ignorance about the specifics of the order, the king directed a copy of the ordinance filed in the archive where the official served. In addition, the commissions of administrative personnel were to spell out precisely the manner in which crown officers were to treat the Indians with whom they had contact. The king warned the officials that their failure to observe the ordinance would result in punishment.[3]

---

[2] Royal Cédula, Madrid, May 31, 1676, Stet. Coll. Escrib. de Cam., Leg. 156, pp. 535-536.

[3] Ibid.

Governor Salazar included a number of orders and recommendations of his own to supplement the royal cédula and to assist Captain Arguelles on his mission. Arguelles was to exercise as much authority and jurisdiction in the conduct of the Visita General as if the governor had gone to Guale to carry out the investigation himself. Specifically, Governor Salazar ordered Captain Arguelles to make a comprehensive investigation of the basic stability of the Guale village political and social structure. The governor deemed this as especially important, for a province with a disturbed populace could not function as a useful ally. Furthermore, Governor Salazar directed Arguelles to make a full inquiry into every aspect of the province regardless of how unimportant a matter might appear to be. If he encountered any irregularity he was to investigate the situation fully and gather all possible evidence, so that the person who committed the offense could be punished. Regarding questions and controversies which arose concerning possession rights to caciqueships, land, and other valuable items which the Indians had, he was to hear both sides of the argument and then render the most equitable decision possible. The governor

expected Captain Arguelles to protect the legitimate as-
pirants fully in their rights. If Arguelles found a situation which he was unable to adjudicate he was to inform
the person or persons concerned that they had the right to
appeal their case to St. Augustine where Governor Salazar
and his subordinates would decide the matter.[4] This intent through the visita to protect the rights of the Indians is a good example of Spanish humanitarianism.

Governor Salazar emphasized the point to Captain
Arguelles that he expected him to exercise a good deal of
caution in the methods which he chose to correct unfavorable conditions extant in Guale. The basic prudence of
the governor is reflected here, for he knew that a hasty
decision or act by Captain Arguelles might precipitate a
rebellion and jeopardize Spanish-Indian relations.[5] Although Governor Salazar cautioned Arguelles to display
discretion in dealing with Indian irregularities, he affirmed that the Captain was to correct any abuses which

---

[4]Titulo de 29 de Noviembre [de 1677] por la descargo, Stet. Coll. Escrib. de Cam., Leg. 156, pp. 519-522.

[5]Ibid. See also Titulo de Visitador de 6 de
Noviembre de 1677, Stet. Coll. Escrib. de Cam., Leg. 156,
pp. 531-533.

existed if they militated against the best interest of the crown and the church. In order to expedite the investigation and to obviate, as nearly as possible, obstacles which the garrison in Guale might pose, Governor Salazar suspended the province lieutenant from office. He stipulated that the suspension was operative from the moment Captain Arguelles entered the province until he departed from Guale.[6]

Captain Arguelles instructions were explicit regarding complaints against the lieutenant, soldiers of the garrison, civilians, Spaniards, mulattoes, Negroes and mestizos. First, he was to investigate the charge to determine the veracity of the Indian complaints. Once Arguelles determined that the charge had a legitimate basis, he was to adjudicate the dispute for Governor Salazar gave him plenary power to exercise in the province.[7]

If a controversy developed with the Franciscan missionaries in Guale, Governor Salazar pointed out that

---

[6] Ibid.

[7] Ibid.

he expected Captain Arguelles to deal with the matter in
an expeditious and mutually beneficial manner. The governor made it clear that the visitador was not to be rigid
in his approach to the problems, for he preferred a prag-
matic solution. With the English enemy so near-by Salazar
did not wish to precipitate discontent with the Franciscans as a result of administrative inflexibility, for he
counted on them to help preserve the status quo in the
province. The governor encouraged Arguelles to display
prudence and tact when he dealt with the friars, so that
neither the interests of the church or crown suffered any
setback. Although Salazar ordered Captain Arguelles to
be flexible when dealing with the Franciscans, he, at the
same time, made it clear that the friars were not to
interfere with civil objectives in the province. To insure that the provincial inhabitants heeded the visitadors
instructions, Governor Salazar stipulated that the Guale
lieutenant, the garrison soldiers, caciques, enijas,
mandadores, herederos, and the Indians were to obey all
decrees that Captain Arguelles issued while in the province. Also Governor Salazar issued a directive that the
Guale inhabitants were to render assistance to Captain

Arguelles whenever he requested it. The governor warned the Indians that if they did not assist Captain Arguelles when needed, that they would be severely punished. Governor Salazar concluded his dispatch by directing Captain Arguelles to look out for the welfare in every instance of the Guale inhabitants.[8]

Although Governor Hita Salazar had selected Captain Arguelles to conduct the Guale investigation, he still had to select a scribe to accompany the expedition. The governor was quite aware of the need which Captain Arguelles would have for a scrivener to take down the official testimony, deliver the numerous oral and written messages, and to prepare the necessary decrees and regulations incident to any type of Spanish investigation. Ordinarily, the governor would have sent the royal scrivener of St. Augustine, Alonso de Solano, to assist Captain Arguelles. However, at this particular time, Governor Salazar had so much official work to do that he was unable to spare him.[9] The governor found that Adjutant Andres

---

[8] Ibid.

[9] Ibid.

de Escobedo, a Reformado,[10] met all the qualifications

necessary for a scribe and nominated him for the position.

Governor Salazar included along with his nomination, spe-

cific instructions for Escobedo to follow in the course

of the investigation. He was to participate in all of the

investigatory proceedings because of the necessity of ob-

taining a complete record. Escobedo was to write down all

the questions that Captain Arguelles asked the Indians and

he was to record fully their replies. So that the general

inspection might be properly conducted, the scrivener was

directed to enter the day, month, and year of all proceed-

ings. He was to insure always that each witness took the

necessary oath before they gave testimony or a deposi-

tion.[11] It is interesting to note that in Governor

Salazar's search for a scribe he "found" that Adjutant

Escobedo was qualified. The search for a scribe seems

---

[10]Nombramiento de Escribano de 29 de Noviembre,
1677, Stet. Coll. Escrib. de Cam., Leg. 156, p. 523;
[Escobedo's Acceptance of the Nomination], November 29,
1677, Stet. Coll. Escrib. de Cam., Leg. 156, p. 524. The
reformado was often a retired soldier who continued to
serve in the absence of a replacement.

[11]Nombramiento de Escribano de 29 de Noviembre,
1677, Stet. Coll. Escrib. de Cam., Leg. 156, p. 523.

simple enough but the Spanish citizenry in seventeenth century Florida were not noted for their educational abilities. Because Florida was a frontier outpost, whose primary purpose was defense, there was no great need for literate people in the area.

As soon as Adjutant Andres de Escobedo indicated his intention to serve Captain Arguelles as his official scribe, the visitador prepared to get his investigation of Guale underway. He traveled immediately to the village, Santa Catalina,[12] situated on St. Catherine's Island, where he promulgated an Auto General de Visita which essentially outlined what the inspecting team hoped to accomplish. Captain Arguelles intended to visit the principal villages of Guale, and he ordered the caciques, enijas, herederos, principales, mandadores, and other

---

[12] Santa Catalina de Guale was located on St. Catherine's off the Georgia coast. See Swanton, Early History of the Creek Indians, p. 80. See also Wenhold (trans.), "A 17th Century Letter of Gabriel Díaz Vara Calderón," pp. 1-14. The population of Santa Catalina at the time was approximately one hundred and forty. See Report of Governor Pablo de Hita Salazar to the King, August 24, 1675, Maynard Geiger, Biographical Dictionary of the Franciscans in Spanish Florida and Cuba, 1528-1541 (Paterson: 1940), p. 129, hereinafter cited as Biographical Dictionary of the Franciscans.

Indians to assemble themselves together in the various
village buhíos to expedite the investigation. The visitador ordered the scribe to read the Auto General de Visita
to the Indians in the villages he visited to explain the
purpose of his visit. The Guale were to apprise Captain
Arguelles of any injustice of which they had any knowledge in the villages or in the provinces. If caciques,
principal men, the Spanish infantrymen, or civilians had
mistreated the Indians, they were to testify about the
injustice. Arguelles encouraged the Guale to inform him
fully about any grievances so that he could endeavor to
correct the situation. He wanted the Indians to know
that he had come to Guale, not to punish them, but to insure that justice and peace prevailed. Specifically, the
visitador wanted to know whether any crimes had occurred
in the province either of a civil or criminal nature, and
he included a section which dealt with the rights and
privileges of the caciques of the Guale villages. He
wished to know in particular if any disputes existed

concerning the suzerainty of the province cacicados.[13]

Regarding the personal conduct of the natives, Captain Arguelles went to great pains to emphasize the fact that he came to the province to investigate not only the public actions of the Indians but their private lives as well. The visitador wanted to know especially whether individuals had committed an offense against the church and the crown or both. To permit disorderly conduct to continue, such as stealing and the maintenance of concubines, could do nothing more than to undermine the basic interests of God and King in the province. Consequently, Captain Arguelles encouraged the Guale Indians to come forth in their village buhíos and to testify against individuals who exceeded the bounds of social propriety. And if the Indians did not know the culprit's name, they could, at least relate all they knew about the event itself. In no case were the Indians to hesitate to inform him about the misconduct of an individual, regardless of whatever social status that person had in the village or

_____

[13]Auto General de Vicita deste Año de 1677, December 20, 1677, Stet. Coll. Escrib. de Cam., Leg. 156, p. 525.

tribe. In performing this service, the Indians acted in the best interests of the church and the state, and it did not mean at all that they testified out of vengence or hatred or as enemies of the people whom they accused.[14]

The final provision of the Auto General de Visita related to customs or tribal rituals which the Guale Indians practiced. In the event that tribal customs gave rise to difficulty in the province, it was the special duty and obligation of the Guale to inform him fully. The visitador assured the Indians that if these customs militated against the best interests of the church and state, he intended to abolish the particular custom or customs or, at the very least, to remove the offensive part or parts of it. An excellent example of this is the fact that the Spaniards permitted the Indians to perform ceremonial dances, but they forbade the Indians to dance "bailes ilicitos," because the Franciscan friars felt that they undermined the teachings of the church. Some customs such as the "juego de pelota" were forbidden altogether. Captain Arguelles promised to help the Indians by providing

---

[14]Ibid.

them with a system of regulations designed to help them maintain an orderly government and live in peace with one another. The visitador directed Andres de Escobedo, the scribe, to read and explain, with the assistance of the interpreter, the Auto General de Visita each time the investigators arrived at an Indian village to conduct its investigation.[15]

On December 21, 1677, Captain Arguelles officially inaugurated the Guale visita when he began the investigation of the village Santa Catalina, forty-four leagues north of St. Augustine. There the village inhabitants assembled in the large council house where Alonso de Escobedo read the Auto General de Visita which the interpreter or ategui,[16] Diego Camunas, explained to them. The village cacique immediately presented a grievance to Captain Arguelles which specifically dealt with the garrison of soldiers stationed in his village. He declared that when the infantrymen first arrived in the province practically all of the Guale caciques and their subjects

[15] Ibid.

[16] The ategui is a Floridismo for interpreter.

had promised to contribute various items such as cassine
(a type of bread) and leather to help out in the maintenance of the garrison. The caciques failed to honor their
commitment, and the Spanish infantrymen received assistance only from the Indians who lived in Santa Catalina.
The village cacique pointed out that the population of his
pueblo had declined since the soldiers arrived, and that
his subjects no longer enjoyed economic prosperity as they
had in former years. As a result, the village inhabitants
found it difficult to furnish food to the soldiers. Although the cacique did not place the blame for the population decline and the economic reversal on the military
in a formal declaration, he subtlely suggested as much
when he declared that his subjects were unable to furnish
much assistance to the military because of their economic
situation at the time. The cacique suggested that it
might be best if Governor Salazar ordered the withdrawal
of the Santa Catalina garrison, but Captain Arguelles
quickly indicated that such a move was not possible. The
Captain did assert however that he intended to require
the other Guale caciques to fulfill their obligations to

the garrison and to take part of the burden off of the natives of Santa Catalina.[17]

Captain Arguelles then turned his attention to a
political question that had developed over the possession
rights to a cacicado. A delegation of caciques and principal men from Satuache,[18] a village located close to the
Edisto River, asked the visitador to settle a succession
problem which arose concerning the cacicado of Faslico,
located apparently in close proximity to Satuache. The
caciques and principal men of Satuache testified that the
cacicado of Faslico had no suzerain as the cacique had
died. Accordingly, they requested the visitador to invest
the suzerainty of the cacicado on an Indian woman by the
name of Lucía. They asserted that the cacicado rightfully
belonged to her. Captain Arguelles agreed to fulfill
their request and ordered that Lucía should be brought

---

[17]Vicita del lugar de Santa Catalina, December 21,
1677, Stet. Coll. Escrib. de Cam., Leg. 156, p. 526.

[18]Swanton located Satuache as being near the Edisto
River, a distance of more than 70 leagues from St. Augus-
tine, but he indicates that they had abandoned the vil-
lage. Probably in 1677 the town lay to the south of the
Savannah River. See Swanton, Early History of the Creek
Indians, p. 61.

before him. Lucía appeared before Captain Arguelles, but
she asserted her female prerogative and declined the position. She asked Arguelles, however, to grant the position
to her sister who was at San Felipe, and who had a legitimate claim to the position. The caciques agreed that such
was the case. With this knowledge, Captain Arguelles
ordered the Guale lieutenant to go to the San Felipe village and to return with Elena which he did and the visitador invested her with the cacicaship of Faslico.[19] The
fact that Captain Arguelles adjudicated the problems of
more than one pueblo while at Santa Catalina is interesting. Not only did he attempt to resolve the difficulties
of Santa Catalina, but he also settled a request by the
inhabitants of Satuache. The fact that the Satuache
caciques and principal men came to Santa Catalina to see
Captain Arguelles did not indicate that Santa Catalina
exercised any degree of sovereignty over the village.
Rather it reflected the fact that Santa Catalina was an
important village in Guale at the time, and thus it was
more convenient for the inhabitants of an obviously minor

---

[19]Vicita del lugar de Santa Catalina, December 21,
1677, Stet. Coll. Escrib. de Cam., Leg. 156, p. 526.

village to come to the pueblo. That Captain Arguelles conferred the sovereignty of the cacicado of Faslico on a woman is not unique but rather it indicated the total absence of a male lineal heir through the matrilinear succession process which normally dictated the candidates for the position.

The Santa Catalina cacique requested one additional favor from Captain Arguelles before the visitador departed. He testified that some of the discontented males of Santa Catalina did nothing but travel incessantly from one village to another. Most of the males were single, but there were some married men who attempted by these wanderings to excape their responsibility to their families. As a result the wives and children lacked many of the necessities of life such as food and adequate shelter. In addition these wandering males caused discipline problems in each village they visited. He asserted to Captain Arguelles that this practice was forbidden some time ago because of the disruptive influence that it had on the province. Captain Arguelles heard the Indian declaration and agreed that wandering from one village to another by the males violated an ordinance which related to the province. The visitador decreed that neither single nor married males were to go from one pueblo to another unless they had specific business that required their trip. Captain Arguelles encouraged the Indians of Guale to help him to enforce this regulation, and he concluded his investigation of the village.[20]

Departing from Santa Catalina, the northernmost of the Spanish outposts, Captain Antonio de Arguelles and his assistants traveled to the pueblo San Joseph de Zapala,[21] forty-two leagues north of St. Augustine, where they conducted the investigation of the town on December 24, 1677. Previously the highest ranking Indians encountered during the visitation had been caciques. At San Joseph, however, Captain Arguelles confronted a female mica by the name of Aanaytasia. In the village council house, there assembled a motley group of individuals before the visitador. In

---

[20] Ibid.

[21] Swanton locates this village "on or near Sapelo Island." See Swanton, Early History of the Creek Indians, p. 89. At the time of the visita there lived about one hundred Indians in the village. See Report of Governor Pablo de Hita Salazar to the King, August 24, 1675, Geiger, Biographical Dictionary of the Franciscans, p. 129. See also Wenhold (trans.), "A 17th Century Letter of Gabriel Díaz Vara Calderón," pp. 1-14.

addition to Mica Aanaytasia, there gathered several caciques, tunaques, mandadores, and both Christian as well as
heathen Indians. This visita assumed at once a lively
characteristic, as the mica, who lived at Tupiqui,[22] a
near-by pueblo, registered a strong complaint to Captain
Arguelles about the caciques and principal men of San
Joseph. The female mica, who obviously resented a loss
of authority, asserted that these tribal leaders were her
vassals, but that they had been insubordinate of late and
had not planted her fields as was their obligation. Felipe, the cacique of San Joseph, vigorously remonstrated
that the Indians had not tilled the mica's fields because
they had not considered themselves as her vassals. And
since the Indians did not believe that Aanaytasia was
their overlord there was no tribal custom or precedent
which obligated them to perform this service for the
Tupiqui mica. Furthermore, Cacique Felipe asserted that
he and his subjects did not intend to render themselves
subservient to Mica Aanaytasia unless someone forced them

---

[22]Tupiqui was located near San Joseph de Zapala.
See Swanton, Early History of the Creek Indians, p. 82.

to do so. This resolute statement confronted Captain Arguelles with no small problem. To avoid further discord, the visitador asserted that he did not wish to make a ruling on this question of suzerainty until he had the opportunity to assemble all the Guale caciques and principal men together to collect their opinions and suggestions on the matter.[23]

Tunaque Alonso then arose to present a personal request to Captain Arguelles. He pointed out that two years earlier Sergeant-Major Nicolas Ponce de León had taken a barbacoa (storage house) of grain away from him when he made a trip to Guale. The barbacoa, Tunaque Alonso asserted, was a gift from the mica who was his aunt. Alonso did not indicate that his aunt was Mica Aanaytasia, but apparently she was the person to whom he referred. Neither did the Tunaque specify to Captain Arguelles the reasons that prompted the Sergeant-Major to deprive him of the barbacoa. Because of the impreciseness of the tunaque's request, Captain Arguelles wondered whether

---

[23]Vicita del lugar de San Joseph de Zapala, December 24, 1677, Stet. Coll. Escrib. de Cam., Leg. 156, pp. 526-527.

some action of Alonso had not caused the Sergeant-Major to
deprive him of the barbacoa.  Finally, the visitador summoned Alonso to inform him that he was returning the barbacoa to him since he did have a legitimate claim to it.
When he informed the tunaque of his decision, Arguelles
implied that he did not believe that the Sergeant-Major
had acted without a legitimate cause.  Accordingly, Captain Arguelles warned Tunaque Alonso that if any further
controversy took place over the barbacoa that it would be
taken away from him.  The assembled tribal leaders had no
other declarations or requests to make to the visitador,
so Captain Arguelles admonished the Indians to keep the
peace among themselves and to be zealous in their devotion
to God and the King.[24]

Captain Arguelles and his investigation team then
traveled southward to conduct the visita of the village
Santo Domingo de Asao,[25] which was thirty-six leagues

---

[24]Ibid., p. 527.

[25]Swanton locates Santo Domingo de Asao either on
St. Simons Island or nearly.  See Swanton, Early History
of the Creek Indians, p. 89.  The population of Santo
Domingo de Asao at the time numbered approximately thirty.
See Report of Governor Pablo de Hita Salazar to the King,

north of St. Augustine, located probably on St. Simon's
Island. When the scribe and the interpreter had completed
their reading and explanation of the Auto General de
Visita, the Indians declared that they had no grievances
to state because no one had mistreated them. Antonio
Sacristan, however, presented a personal request to the
visitador. He asked Captain Arguelles to grant him possession of the cacicado of Yfulo. Sacristan supported
his request with the statement that at the time there was
no cacique to govern the inhabitants of the cacicado. In
addition, he swore that he was the legitimate heredero
and that the pueblo caciqueship properly belonged to him.
Captain Arguelles consulted with the assembled Indians in
an effort to determine if Antonio had a legitimate claim
to the cacicado. The Indians told Captain Arguelles that
the former cacique of Yfulo declared before his demise
that the cacicado rightfully belonged to Juan Ysape and
not to Antonio Sacristan. Armed with this valuable evidence, the visitador did not honor Sacristan's petition,

---

August 24, 1675, Geiger, Biographical Dictionary of the
Franciscans, p. 129. See also Wenhold (trans.), "A 17th
Century Letter of Gabriel Díaz Vara Calderón," pp. 1-14.

but he was unable to confer the caciqueship on Juan Ysape

for, at the time, Ysape was not present in the village.

Captain Arguelles, after encouraging the Indians to live

in peace and to heed the mandates of God and King, con-

cluded the village's inspection.[26]

On December 30, 1677, Captain Arguelles inaugurated

the general investigation of Mocama, a subdivision of

Guale. The Mocama Indians spoke the Timucuan dialect but

for administrative purposes they were considered as a part

of Guale.[27] Since the Indians of Mocama spoke the Timu-

cuan language, Captain Arguelles had to secure another in-

terpreter. Consequently, he nominated Juan Martín, proba-

bly a native of the area who spoke Spanish, for the posi-

tion, and he dispatched Andres de Escobedo to notify him

of the appointment.[28] Juan Martín accepted Captain

---

[26]Vicita del lugar de Santo Domingo de Asao, December 28, 1677, Stet. Coll. Escrib. de Cam., Leg. 156,
p. 527.

[27]The Spanish referred to these Indian towns as
part of the province of "Guale y Mocamo." See Swanton,
Early History of the Creek Indians, p. 322.

[28]Nombramiento de atequi en los lugares de la
Mocama, December 30, 1677, Stet. Coll. Escrib. de Cam.,
Leg. 156, pp. 527-528; Aceptación y Juramento, December
30, 1677, Stet. Coll. Escrib. de Cam., Leg. 156, p. 528.

Arguelles' nomination immediately and the following day,
Captain Arguelles began the investigation of San Buenaventura de Ovedalquini which was located on Jekyl Island,
approximately thirty leagues north of St. Augustine.[29]
Both the Christian and non-Christian caciques told the
visitador that they lived peacefully with each other, and
that no one had offended or mistreated them. Captain
Arguelles admonished the Christian caciques to continue
rendering their obedience to God and King, and he encouraged the heathen caciques to emulate the examples of
the Christian chiefs. The Captain informed all of the
caciques that they were to keep a constant vigilance
against enemy intrusions into the province. He ordered
the Indians to maintain an especially diligent watch on
the ports of the province to guard against illegal trade
operations that the Carolinians might attempt to inaugurate. As the Indians had nothing else to say, Arguelles

---

[29]Swanton locates San Buenaventura de Ovadalquini
on Jekyl Island. See Swanton, Early History of the Creek
Indians, p. 90. San Buenaventura had approximately forty
individuals at the time of the Visita General. See Report of Governor Pablo de Hita Salazar to the King, August
24, 1675, Geiger, Biographical Dictionary of the Franciscans, p. 129. See also Wenhold (trans.), "A 17th Century Letter of Gabriel Díaz Vara Calderón," pp. 1-14.

concluded the inspection of the pueblo, and resumed the in-

spection of the villages which spoke the Guale dialect.[30]

January 3, 1678, Captain Arguelles inaugurated the

visita of San Felipe,[31] twenty-one leagues north of St.

Augustine, and since the visita team had returned to

pueblos which spoke the Guale dialect, Diego Camunas

served once again as the interpreter. The caciques and

principal men heard the Auto General de Visita and they

had no statement or declaration to make, for they lived

in harmony with one another; and no one had mistreated

them. Arguelles concluded the visita of San Felipe[32] and

---

[30]Vicita del lugar de [San Buenaventura] de
Ovadalquini, December 31, 1677, Stet. Coll. Escrib. de
Cam., Leg. 156, p. 528.

[31]Wenhold (trans.), "A 17th Century Letter of
Gabriel Díaz Vara Calderón," pp. 1-14; Report of Governor Pablo de Hita Salazar to the King, August 24, 1675,
Geiger, Biographical Dictionary of the Franciscans, p.
129. The population at the time numbered about thirty-
six persons. See also Jonathan Dickinson, Narrative of
a Shipwreck in the Gulf of Florida: Showing God's Protecting Providence, Man's Surest Help and Defence in
Times of Greatest Difficulty, and Most Imminent Danger
(Burlington: Lexington Press, 1811), p. 93, hereinafter
cited as Dickinson, Narrative of a Shipwreck.

[32]Vicita en el lugar de San Felipe, January 3,
1678, Stet. Coll. Escrib. de Cam., Leg. 156, p. 529.

traveled to the pueblo Santa María de los Yamasis,[33] eighteen leagues north of St. Augustine. There he carried out the inspection January 5, 1678. When Diego Camunas had finished his interpretation of the Auto General de Visita, Cacique Finge informed Captain Arguelles that he had abandoned his cacicado because his subjects had become rebellious and no longer obeyed him. Arguelles told the cacique that he should return to his cacicado and that he would work with him in reestablishing the proper respect among the vassals. Once this had been done, if an Indian refused to respect the cacique he was to be carried as a prisoner to St. Augustine where the governor would determine his punishment. There being no further business, Captain Arguelles departed from Santa Maria.[34]

---

[33]Wenhold (trans.), "A 17th Century Letter of Gabriel Díaz Vara Calderón," pp. 1-14; Report of Governor Pablo de Hita Salazar to the King, August 24, 1675, Geiger, Biographical Dictionary of the Franciscans, p. 129. There lived approximately forty persons in the village at the time of the arrival of Arguelles. See also Dickinson, Narrative of a Shipwreck, pp. 92-93.

[34]Vicita del lugar de Santa María de los Yamasis, January 5, 1678, Stet. Coll. Escrib. de Cam., Leg. 156, p. 529.

January 8, 1678, Captain Antonio de Arguelles conducted the visita of San Juan del Puerto,[35] which was located twelve leagues north of St. Augustine. The Indians here spoke the Timucuan dialect, and the visitador pressed Juan Martín into service again. The only problem which Arguelles encountered here was one of succession in the pueblo leadership. Juana Meléndez, the cacica of the pueblo, expressed a desire to step down from the cacicaship because of her age. She asked the Captain to confer her title on her niece Merensiana who was the legitimate heir to the cacicaship. The other caciques, who had assembled in the council house, declared that Juana Meléndez had spoken the truth, and Captain Arguelles conferred the cacicaship upon Merensiana and concluded his inspection of the pueblo.[36]

---

[35]See Wenhold (trans.), "A 17th Century Letter of Gabriel Díaz Vara Calderón," pp. 1-14. See also Report of Governor Pablo de Hita Salazar to the King, August 24, 1675, Geiger, Biographical Dictionary of the Franciscans, p. 129. There lived in the village approximately thirty persons at the time. See also Dickinson, Narrative of a Shipwreck, pp. 91-92.

[36]Vicita [de] San Juan del Puerto, January 8, 1678, Stet. Coll. Escrib. de Cam., Leg. 156, pp. 529-530.

Visitador Arguelles concluded the visita of Guale
and Mocama at the pueblo Nuestra Señora de Guadalupe de
Tolomato,[37] two leagues north of St. Augustine on January
10, 1678. After Diego Camunas had finished interpreting
the Auto General de Visita, the mica and his fellow
caciques and principal men testified that they lived at
peace with one another, and that they had no statements
or complaints to make. Thereupon, Captain Arguelles
ordered the caciques to treat their subjects well and to
be obedient vassals to God and the Crown.[38]

Shortly afterwards, Antonio Arguelles returned to
the Florida capital. Altogether, the investigation of
Guale had required twenty-one days. During this relatively short span of time, Captain Arguelles had conducted
investigations in eight villages. In six of them, the
Guale language predominated, but in two towns, San Buenaventura de Ovedalquini and San Juan del Puerto, the

---

[37][La Natividad de] Nuestra Señora de [Guadalupe
de] Tolomato was located approximately two leagues north
of St. Augustine. See Wenhold (trans.), "A 17th Century
Letter of Gabriel Díaz Vara Calderón," pp. 1-14.

[38]Vicita [de la Natividad de] Nuestra Señora de
[Guadalupe] de Tolomato, January 10, 1678, Stet. Coll.
Escrib. de Cam., Leg. 156, p. 530.

Indians spoke the Timucuan dialect. Arguelles did not visit by any means all of the Guale villages, but he did conduct investigations of the principal towns in the province. It is an interesting fact that Captain Arguelles chose to begin the Visita General at Santa Catalina, the northernmost Guale town of significance and to work southward. Perhaps it is best explained in light of the fact that the Guale garrison was stationed here and this was the best place to begin an inquiry into the subject of Spanish-Indian relations.

## CHAPTER VII

## SERGEANT-MAJOR DOMINGO DE LETURIONDO'S VISITA

## GENERAL OF APALACHEE, DECEMBER 22, 1677

## TO JANUARY 10, 1678

Simultaneously with the decision to send Captain
Arguelles to inspect Guale, Governor Pablo Hita Salazar determined to send an investigating team to conduct a Visita
General in the provinces of Timucua and Apalachee.  He set
forth as his primary reason the necessity to maintain an
orderly government in the area.  Incident to orderly provinces was the need for converting as many of the Indians
as possible.  Spaniards who had traveled in these provinces, upon returning to St. Augustine, had indicated
that the Timucuan and Apalachee Indians were restless.
Since administrative duties dictated against a personal
visit to the provinces, the governor turned to the St.
Augustine garrison to secure a competent replacement.  He
knew that Sergeant-Major Domingo de Leturiondo was fully
qualified to serve as a substitute visitador, and picked

him to carry out the general inspection of Timucua and
Apalachee.[1]

The governor gave Sergeant-Major Domingo de
Leturiondo essentially the same authority and power to
conduct the investigation that he gave to Captain
Arguelles for the Guale visita. Governor Salazar cautioned the Sergeant-Major to use discretion in the ap-
plication of decrees and to put into force whatever
augured best for the good government and the welfare of
the villages and the provinces. The visitador was given
the authority to reward and punish Indians. The visita
was to relate to general and particular matters, and when
the Sergeant-Major discovered an irregularity he was to
investigate the matter fully, collecting all the evidence
extant, in order to bring offenders to justice and punish
them for their misconduct. In each case, however, he was
to inform those individuals that they had the opportunity,
if they chose, to appeal their case at St. Augustine. The
governor instructed the Sergeant-Major that when controversies developed over possession rights of cacicados,

---

[1]Titulo de Visitador de 6 de Noviembre de 1677,
Stet. Coll. Escrib. de Cam., Leg. 156, pp. 531-534.

lands, and other valuables he was to listen carefully to the arguments of the litigants and seek always to protect the rights of the legitimate owner or aspirant. Governor Salazar made it clear that he expected Sergeant-Major Leturiondo to exercise a good deal of caution in suppressing tribal abuses, for some of the abuses or irregularities which the Indians practiced dated back to ancient times. Irrespective of the antiquity of the custom, he ordered the Sergeant-Major to put an end to the customs if they violated ecclesiastical or governmental precepts.[2]

Governor Salazar suspended the lieutenants of Apalachee from the performance of their duties to enable Sergeant-Major Leturiondo to conduct his investigation without impediments. The suspension became operative when the Sergeant-Major arrived in Apalachee province, and was to be lifted when he departed from the area. The governor included one stipulation not in Captain Arguelles' instructions which prescribed the manner in which the visitador was to handle complaints the Indians made against the province lieutenant. Sergeant-Major

---

[2]_Ibid._

Leturiondo was not to settle any complaints against the lieutenant, rather he was to send them to St. Augustine for Governor Salazar to render a decision. The governor ordered Sergeant-Major Leturiondo to begin his Visita General of Apalachee in San Luis de Talimali,[3] approximately eighty-nine leagues west of St. Augustine, and from there he was to proceed to the other villages in the province.[4]

Governor Salazar knew that the Sergeant-Major could possibly run into difficulty on the visita with some of the Franciscan friars. Accordingly, the governor desired, for the purpose of province harmony to avoid altogether or to minimize, at least, any church-crown difficulty. He gave Leturiondo freedom of action in the decisions that

---

[3] San Luis de Talimali was located near Tallahassee, Florida. The site has been excavated and the results are published in Mark F. Boyd, Hale G. Smith, and John W. Griffin, Here They Once Stood: The Tragic End of the Apalachee Missions (Gainesville: University of Florida Press, 1951). See also Wenhold (trans.), "A 17th Century Letter of Gabriel Díaz Vara Calderón," pp. 1-14. See also Report of Governor Pablo de Hita Salazar to the King, August 24, 1675, Geiger, Biographical Dictionary of the Franciscans, p. 130. The population of San Luis was approximately 1,400 at the time.

[4] Titulo de Visitador de 6 de Noviembre de 1677, Stet. Coll. Escrib. de Cam., Leg. 156, pp. 531-534.

he was to make in the event that a controversy arose.

However, he did not expect the Sergeant-Major to do any-

thing which might damage the interest of the Catholic

Church and the Spanish Crown in that area.  In no case,

however, was the Sergeant-Major to allow the Franciscan

friars to obstruct the execution of a decision that he

made for the general welfare of the province.  Sergeant-

Major Leturiondo, to be sure, was to cooperate fully with

the padres in every possible way, but he was to make the

point clear that the primary authority for the province

resided with the Crown.[5]

Governor Salazar decreed that the lieutenants in

Timucua and Apalachee, the soldiers under their command

and any other Spaniards in the area, caciques, enijas,

mandadores, herederos, and other Indians were to obey all

the orders and regulations that the Sergeant-Major gave

them.  In addition, the governor expected these indivi-

duals to assist Sergeant-Major Leturiondo in any task in

which he required their assistance.  Those who failed in

this respect were to receive severe punishment.  Salazar

---

[5]Ibid.

ordered the Sergeant-Major to treat the Indians well and
to insure that no one mistreated them.[6]

In San Luis de Talimali, December 18, 1677, the
Sergeant-Major promulgated an Auto General para la Visita
in which he set forth the purpose and intent of the visita
which he was about to begin.  The general decree stipulated that all the Indians of Apalachee and Timucua were
to assemble themselves in their council houses when the
Sergeant-Major came to visit their villages.  Sergeant-
Major Leturiondo concluded that by congregating the Indians in one central place, he could expedite the inspection
of the province.  He intended to inform the Indians in the
council house of the authority which Governor Hita Salazar
had invested in him, and he determined to inform the
caciques and their vassals that their province lieutenants
were suspended from their offices for the duration of the
investigation.  Thus, he sought to assure the Indians that
they need not fear to say that the lieutenant or the garrison soldiers mistreated them.  The Auto General encouraged the Indians to speak out if any Spaniard had

---

[6]Ibid.

bothered or mistreated them so that the offender could be punished.[7]

Sergeant-Major Leturiondo did his best in the Auto General to assure the Indians that he came to their province to guarantee law and order to all inhabitants. He encouraged the Indians to present all grievances and complaints, large or small. The visitador wished to know not only about the complaints they had against the Spaniards, he desired to know about the disputes which the Indians had among themselves. Leturiondo considered the possession rights of cacicados, scandals (the maintenance of concubines), the failure of neophytes to attend mass and to obey their tribal leaders as important areas which warranted thorough investigation. He reminded the Indians of their especial duty to God and the king and that as loyal subjects it was their duty to inform him fully if any irregularities existed in the villages or the provinces. Their statements, he observed, portended benefits not only for the church and the Spanish crown, but they helped also to improve conditions in their own villages and the

---

[7] Auto [General para la Vicita] San Luis de Talimali, Stet. Coll. Escrib. de Cam., Leg. 156, p. 537.

province. The inhabitants were not to think of themselves as informers motivated by anger and enmity, but rather they were to consider that they exercised the serious responsibility of good citizens interested in the welfare of their homes and villages. Sergeant-Major Leturiondo urged the Indians to give him complete and accurate testimony. He ordered the Auto General read in each of the villages and dispatched the Scribe Lorenzo de la Bora to inform the province lieutenant of his suspension from office.[8]

December 19, 1677, Leturiondo chose two interpreters to assist him in the provinces. He selected Juan Bautista de la Cruz, a presidio soldier stationed at St. Augustine, to interpret the Timucuan language, and Diego de Salvador to serve him in Apalachee. The same day, Lorenzo de la Bora notified the interpreters of their appointments and they took the oath to exercise faithfully the duties of the office.[9] December 20, 1677, Sergeant-Major Leturiondo issued an Auto which ordered all the

[8]Ibid., p. 538.

[9]Auto [Nomination of the Interpreter], December 19, 1677, Stet. Coll. Escrib. de Cam., Leg. 156, p. 539; Aceptación y Juramento, December 19, 1677, Stet. Coll. Escrib. de Cam., Leg. 156, pp. 539-540.

caciques and principal men of Apalachee province to assemble on Wednesday, December 22, in the pueblo, San Martín de Tomoli,[10] located approximately two leagues west of San Luis. Sergeant-Major Leturiondo intended to have a Junta General with all of the various village leaders to discuss matters which pertained to the general welfare of the province.

The caciques and the principal men gathered in the council house at San Martín on the designated day, and the visitador invited them to make, if they wished, opening statements or declarations about the general condition of the province. The Indians conferred among themselves, and replied with unanimity that they did not have anything to report at the time. They did indicate, however, that they intended to make representations when the visitador came to their individual villages. Leturiondo told the Indian leaders of his decision to ban the ball game in the

---

[10]Auto, December 20, 1677, Stet. Coll. Escrib. de Cam., Leg. 156, p. 540; Wenhold (trans.), "A 17th Century Letter of Gabriel Díaz Vara Calderón," pp. 1-14. See also Report of Governor Pablo de Hita Salazar to the King, August 24, 1675, Geiger, Biographical Dictionary of the Franciscans, p. 730. The population of San Martín at the time was approximately seven hundred.

provinces because it was so dangerous and because certain aspects of it apparently reflected pagan rather than Christian precepts. He realized the game was an ancient custom and regretted the necessity to suspend the sport. The material as well as the spiritual welfare of the provinces permitted no other course of action.[11]

Leturiondo informed the Indians that he knew that certain of the Apalachee disapproved of his action in this matter for the discontented Indians not only disapproved, they complained about his decision in the province. The Sergeant-Major declared that since most of the villages had representatives at San Martín, that he intended to find out the sentiments of each pueblo about the matter. He indicated his desire to discuss thoroughly the merits of the ball game so that a final decision could be reached. If the caciques and their subjects agreed, as he had, that the sport had sufficient abuses to condemn it, then he had no recourse but to order the game prohibited for all time. Conversely, if they showed him that

---

[11] Auto, December 20, 1677, Stet. Coll. Escrib. de Cam., Leg. 156, p. 540; [Junta General, San Martín de] Tomoli, December 22, 1677, Stet. Coll. Escrib. de Cam., Leg. 156, pp. 540-541.

the sport did not have adverse aspects, then he intended
to permit the Indians to resume playing the game. The
Sergeant-Major made it patently clear, however, that whatever decision they reached had to harmonize with the best
interest of catholicism and the Spanish Crown. Leturiondo
proceeded to take a poll of the village caciques. All of
the caciques declared that the decision to suppress the
game was justified. They acknowledged that the game had
abuses, and they agreed that portions of it reflected a
pagan origin. They finished their declaration about the
evils of the ball game, and the visitador issued an order
which banned the sport in the province permanently.[12] Because of the fact that the ball game was an old custom,
the question arose as to how much the Indians really appreciated the suppression of their principal form of
recreation.

Prior to the beginning of the visita the villages
of Apalachee had engaged in a war against the heathen
Chisca Indians. The Chiscas harrassed the Apalachees by

---

[12] [Junta General, San Martín de] Tomoli, December
22, 1677, Stet. Coll. Escrib. de Cam., Leg. 156, pp. 541-
542.

raiding their villages and carrying off their women and children to serve them as slaves. Tired of these alien intrusions and depredations, the Apalachees had decided to make war on them. Captain Juan Fernández de Florencia, the province lieutenant, granted permission to the Apalachees to go against the Chiscas, and he provided ammunition for those Apalachee Indians who possessed arquebuses. The Sergeant-Major expressed his personal thanks to the caciques and warriors who participated in the expedition against the Chiscas, and he encouraged the Apalachees to display always this type of loyalty to the crown and church whenever they had the opportunity. Leturiondo ordered the Apalachee when they went into battle not to kill the women and children captives. Rather, he emphasized to the Indians the necessity of sparing their lives and attempting to convert them.[13] An unusual aspect of the campaign against the Chiscas is the

---

[13]Swanton, Early History of the Creek Indians, p. 119; Juan Fernández de Florencia to Governor Salazar, August 30, 1678, Serrano y Sanz (ed.), Documentos Historicos de la Florida y la Luisiana Siglos XVI al XVIII, pp. 207-216; [Junta General, San Martín de] Tomoli, December 22, 1677, Stet. Coll. Escrib. de Cam., Leg. 156, p. 542.

fact that the province lieutenant furnished ammunition for the Apalachee arquebusiers. As a rule Spain did not furnish weapons to her Indian subjects. This particular deviation from established practice is interesting and raises the question as to whether this possession of weapons was an isolated instance or whether the Spaniards, plagued by inadequate numbers of soldiers, distributed weapons in Apalachee to bolster the defensive force.

Two days later, December 24, Sergeant-Major Leturiondo began his investigation of the Apalachee pueblos. The visitador ordered the caciques, principal men, and other Indians of San Martín de Tomoli to assemble in the council house. Diego Salvador, the interpreter, read and explained the Auto General de Visita to them, and the Indians informed the Sergeant-Major that they understood what he expected of them. The interpreter read the Auto to the Indians a second time. Since the Indians had no grievances or complaints to present, Leturiondo traveled immediately to Nuestra Señora de la Candelaria de la Tama, located approximately one league northwest of San Luis, where he conducted an investigation that afternoon. Salvador read and explained the Auto General to the

Indians. The village inhabitants had no testimony to give, so the visita team departed[14] to investigate San Luis de Talimali.

The lieutenant of the province, Juan Fernández de Florencia lived in San Luis which was located approximately eighty-nine leagues west of St. Augustine. December 26, 1677, Diego Salvador read the Auto to the assembled Indians. The Apalachees indicated that no disputes existed in their village of a nature that compelled them to report it to the Sergeant-Major. In addition, they had no complaints to utter against Captain Juan Fernández de Florencia, the province lieutenant, for he had treated them well. They admitted that whenever they

---

[14][Auto to assemble the inhabitants of San Martín de] Tomoli, December 24, 1677, Stet. Coll. Escrib. de Cam., Leg. 156, pp. 542-543; Auto [de San Martín de] Tomoli, December 24, 1677, Stet. Coll. Escrib. de Cam., Leg. 156, p. 543; Wenhold (trans.), "A 17th Century Letter of Gabriel Díaz Vara Calderón," pp. 1-14; [Auto to assemble the inhabitants of Nuestra Señora de la Candelaria de la] Tama, December 24, 1677, Stet. Coll. Escrib. de Cam., Leg. 156, pp. 543-544; Auto [de Nuestra Señora de la Candelaria de la] Tama, December 24, 1677, Stet. Coll. Escrib. de Cam., Leg. 156, p. 544; Report of Governor Pablo de Hita Salazar to the King, August 24, 1675, Geiger, Biographical Dictionary of the Franciscans, p. 130. The population of the pueblo was approximately three hundred.

brought a dispute for him to adjudicate that he settled

the matter as equitably as possible. The Indians informed

Leturiondo that from time to time Spaniards came to

Apalachee from Havana and St. Augustine, but that they

had not harmed or mistreated them in any way. The San

Luis Indians expressed their opinion that the Sergeant-

Major acted wisely when he suppressed the ball game, for

the sport had evil features, and they realized that the

visitador prohibited the game only because he had their

best interests and welfare in mind. Leturiondo settled

some minor disputes which the Scribe did not record, and

concluded the pueblo's visita.[15]

Prior to his departure from San Luis, the Sergeant-

Major adjudicated a matter which pertained to the port at

St. Marks. Captain Juan de la Rosa of the frigate La

Natividad y San Francisco came before him to make a state-

ment. Rosa testified that prior to the arrival of the

visitador a group of English renegades had slipped into

---

[15][Auto to assemble the inhabitants of] San Luis,
December 26, 1677, Stet. Coll. Escrib. de Cam., Leg.
156, pp. 544-545; Auto, San Luis de Talimali, December
26, 1677, Stet. Coll. Escrib. de Cam., Leg. 156, pp. 545-
546.

the harbor at St. Marks and stolen a vessel which belonged to the Alférez Diego de Florencia of Havana which had been intrusted to him. Not only did the pirates make away with the vessel, they took the ship's cargo and the contents of a storage house on the wharf. The storage house contained tools, a chest of amber, doeskins, and other items. Captain Rosa declared that he was fortunate to escape from the pirates, and asked the visitador not to punish him for having lost the ship and the cargo.[16] Captain Antonio Francisco de Herrera, the commandant at San Marcos, also appeared before the visitador, and his testimony substantiated Captain Rosa's declaration.[17] He also identified the maurauders as English sailors. In addition, the province lieutenant Captain Juan Fernández de Florencia, Friar Francisco de Medina, and Friar Juan de Mercado swore that Captain Rosa spoke the truth. The Sergeant-Major listened to all of the testimony and decided that Captain

---

[16]Declaration of Captain Juan de la Roza, December 24, 1677, Stet. Coll. Escrib. de Cam., Leg. 156, p. 584.

[17]Testimony of Captain Antonio Francisco de Herrera, December 24, 1677, Stet. Coll. Escrib. de Cam., Leg. 156, p. 585.

Rosa deserved no punishment.[18]

Sergeant-Major Domingo de Leturiondo traveled from San Luis de Talimali to the village San Cosme y San Damián de Cupaica, located approximately one league due north of San Luis. There, on December 28, the visitador ordered the natives to assemble in the council house and the interpreter explained the Auto General to the Indians. The following day, Diego de Salvador explained the Auto to them again, and Lorenzo de la Bora prepared to take down their answers and declarations to the Sergeant-Major's questions. The Indians had no grievances to present, but Nicolas Tafunsaca, an enija who lived in the hearby village of Yfalcasar, stepped forward to present a personal request.[19]

---

[18] Statements of Captain Juan Fernández de Florencia, Fray Francisco de Medina and Fray Juan de Mercado, December 24, 1677, Stet. Coll. Escrib. de Cam., Leg. 156, pp. 585-586.

[19] Wenhold (trans.), "A 17th Century Letter of Gabriel Díaz Vara Calderón," pp. 1-14; Nota de las misiones de la provincia de la Florida, establecidos por los Franciscos observantes en 1655, con un convento en la capital a donde se recogian los misioneros enfermos, sin otros pueblos de conversion agregados, y demas que estaban a cargo de derigos Seculares, Serrano y Sanz, Documentos Historicos de la Florida y la Luisiana Siglos XVI

Nicolas testified that he was the legitimate heir
of the cacicado of Yfalcasar, a pueblo under the suzerainty of San Cosme y San Damían. His testimony indicated that Osunaca Pedro García usurped his legitimate
inheritance, and that he did it in a most despicable way.
Nicolas Tafunsaca testified to the visitador that Osunaca
Pedro García had seized the caciqueship eight years
earlier upon the death of his uncle, Cacique Tafunsaca
Martín. He did this when Nicolas and his brother, who
had first claim on the caciqueship, were absent from the
pueblo. During their absence, Osunaca Pedro García assumed the caciqueship through illegal means. Osunaca
Pedro García had served the deceased Cacique Tafunsaca
Martin as a principal man in the village heirarchy. As
such, he acquired a good deal of prestige and developed
a considerable following. In addition, he exerted considerable influence over the other principal men of the
cacicado. Osunaca Pedro García immediately decided to

---

al XVIII, pp. 132-133; Report of Governor Pablo de Hita
Salazar to the King, August 24, 1675, Geiger, Biographical Dictionary of the Franciscans, p. 130. The population of the pueblo at the time was approximately one
hundred.

establish himself as the new cacique upon Cacique Tafunsaca Martín's demise and to present the legal aspirant, Tafunsaca Feliciano, with an accomplished fact when he returned. Accordingly, Osunaca Pedro García hurriedly called the three other principal men of the village together in a hasty attempt to provide a facade of legality for his spurious pretension. Osunaca Pedro García took great pains to point out to his fellow principal men that they had an excellent opportunity to grasp control of village affairs and to concentrate their direction in their hands alone.[20]

Accordingly, he urged the principal men to say that they had chosen him as the new cacique for the pueblo of Yfalcasar. He assured them that if they supported him in his plan that they would have privileged places under his administration. And he warned the principal men if they failed to follow through on his request, that Tafunsaca Feliciano was certain to gain the caciqueship and that they had no chance to exercise more than ordinary

---

[20] [San Cosme y San Damián de] Cupaica Auto, December 29, 1677, Stet. Coll. Escrib. de Cam., Leg. 156, pp. 547-549.

influence in pueblo affairs. Osunaca Pedro García reminded the village elders that Tafunsaca Feliciano lived in a very profligate manner as a young man. On one occasion he had shot some of the villagers' hogs with arrows, which in itself reflected irresponsibility not needed in a village cacique. Such a man, Osunaca Pedro García suggested, forfeited his hereditary right to serve as the cacique. Osunaca Pedro García hinted strongly that Tafunsaca Feliciano did not mature with age, and he urged the principal men to declare himself as the village cacique. The principal men assented to his request and informed the province lieutenant that the legitimate heir to the caciqueship was Osunaca Pedro García, and that Tafunsaca Feliciano's claim was false.[21]

Nicolas Tafunsaca testified that Osunaca Pedro García and his cohorts usurped the caciqueship and totally ignored the fact that the old cacique, Tafunsaca Martín, had indicated before his death that Feliciano and he were his legitimate heirs. In essence the action of Osunaca Pedro García and the principal men constituted the most

---

[21]Ibid.

flagrant violation of justice, for there were witnesses who heard Tafunsaca Martín's statement. Bernardo Ynachuba, the cacique of San Cosme y San Damían de Cupaica, and Tafunsaca Bautista, the interpreter of the church, were present when the Reverend Father Domingo Padura came to administer extreme unction to the dying cacique. They heard Tafunsaca Martín's testimony that Tafunsaca Feliciano and Tafunsaca Nicolas were the legal heirs to the cacicado.[22]

Sergeant-Major Leturiondo listened attentively to Tafunsaca Nicolas' statement and ordered the Indians to assemble again in the council house to question them about the veracity of his testimony. The village inhabitants testified that Tafunsaca Nicolas spoke the truth. Even the spurious cacique, Osunaca Pedro García, in the face of this mass of testimony, admitted that Nicolas was the legitimate cacique and that he had usurped the position as charged. In the light of this testimony, Sergeant-Major Leturiondo deprived Osunaca Pedro García of his position and installed Tafunsaca Nicolas as the cacique

---

[22] _Ibid._

of Yfalcasar, since his brother, Tafunsaca Feliciano, had died.[23]

Leturiondo decided, in the interest of the village harmony, to banish Osunaca Pedro García from the area. Since he was an old man, he ruled out severe punishment, and only required him to pay a fine of twelve measures of corn to the province lieutenant. Simultaneously, Leturiondo ordered Captain Florencia to use the food to feed transient individuals who came to Apalachee. The Sergeant-Major did not punish the three principal men who assisted Osunaca Pedro García in his quest for the caciqueship since they were dead. Before concluding the matter of the cacicado, Leturiondo asked Tafunsaca Nicolas why he had waited eight years to present his case. Nicolas answered that it was his brother's responsibility to do this. The brother, Tafunsaca Feliciano, had not brought the question before the province lieutenant, for he felt that he would not receive justice. Tafunsaca Nicolas indicated that he did not share his brother's pessimistic views and that upon his recent demise that

---

[23]Ibid.

he had decided to present the facts so that the visitador would confirm him with the title and he would thereby gain his legitimate inheritance.[24]

Visitador Leturiondo turned his attention to a question regarding the youth of San Damían. He observed regretfully that no facilities existed in the village to instruct the village children in the rudiments of reading and writing. Consequently, the Sergeant-Major ordered the inhabitants of the cacicado to plant a field to provide food for a teacher he intended to acquire for the village and to assist him in any tasks which required assistance. The Sergeant-Major alerted the province lieutenant of the need to visit the village from time to time to see how well the educational plan was carried out.[25] Leturiondo did not specify whether the teacher should be a lay or religious person. It was highly probable that it was a Franciscan, for few individuals besides the friars and military officers possessed the necessary educational background to serve as teachers.

---

[24] Ibid.

[25] Ibid.

The Sergeant-Major then dealt with a problem which occurred with sufficient frequency that it threatened to undermine pueblo harmony unless curbed. Specifically, Leturiondo ordered the San Damían inhabitants to refuse entrance in their village to single and married Indian males from other villages in the province, unless they carried written permission from the lieutenant at San Luis. He amplified on this matter by pointing out that frequently these individuals did nothing but wander about the province and create disciplinary problems in the various pueblos. More often than not, they departed from their own villages in a deliberate effort to avoid work and other responsibilities. Their very presence contributed nothing to the welfare of other villages, and he ordered the Indians to expel them if any sought entrance. Leturiondo directed the scribe to promulgate the order in all the towns in the province to put an end to the difficulty caused by wandering Indians. He warned the caciques that if they permitted an Indian to come into their village without the lieutenant's written permission that they had to pay a fine of twelve doeskins or the equivalent value. There were no other matters to discuss, so the Sergeant-Major concluded his inspection of the village and departed for San Antonio de Bacuqua, which was located approximately three leagues northeast of San Luis.[26]

The visitador arrived in San Antonio de Bacuqua on December 30, 1677. Lorenzo de la Bora and Diego Salvador set to work immediately to assemble the Indians in the council house, where Salvador interpreted for them the Auto General. Leturiondo conducted the visita of the pueblo the following day. The Indians spoke nothing but the highest praise for Captain Juan Fernández de Florencia. Every time they came before him, he had acted kindly toward them and had done his best to settle their problems in an equitable manner. Non-resident Spaniards who sometimes came to Apalachee from Havana and St. Augustine had not mistreated them either. The Indians expressed their appreciation to the Sergeant-Major for suppressing the ball game. They affirmed that they spoke out against the "juego de pelota" at San Martín de Tomoli, and that they had not changed their minds. All of them agreed that the

---

[26]Ibid.

Sergeant-Major acted for the welfare of the province when
he prohibited the game.[27]

Leturiondo moved from a discussion of the ball game
to a consideration of the educational resources of the
pueblo. Evidently not pleased with the conditions in San
Antonio, he directed the natives to establish a school and
to assist the person who came to teach the children in any
way possible. As in the case of San Damián, Sergeant-
Major Leturiondo cautioned the Indians about the large
number of Indian males who wandered about the province
creating trouble, and told them to turn these bachelors
and fugitive husbands away from their village if they
failed to present a written authorization to travel in
the province.[28]

Sergeant-Major Leturiondo traveled from San Antonio

---

[27] Wenhold (trans.), "A 17th Century Letter of
Gabriel Díaz Vara Calderón," pp. 1-14; [Auto to assemble
the inhabitants of San Antonio de] Bacuqua, December 30,
1677, Stet. Coll. Escrib. de Cam., Leg. 156, p. 550; Report of Governor Pablo de Hita Salazar to the King, August
24, 1675, Geiger, Biographical Dictionary of the Franciscans, p. 130. The population of the village was about
one hundred and twenty at the time.

[28] Auto [de San Antonio de] Bacuqua, December 31,
1677, Stet. Coll. Escrib. de Cam., Leg. 156, pp. 550-551.

to San Pedro y San Pablo de Patali which was located approximately two leagues northeast of San Antonio. Lorenzo
de la Bora and Diego de Salvador gathered the Indians together in their council house on December 31, 1677, and
Diego Salvador, the atequi, explained the Auto General to
the natives. The Indians had no statements or declarations to make. Since they had no problems which might
occupy his time, Visitador Leturiondo, as in the case of
the other villages, ordered them to start a school for
their children, to furnish food for the teacher, and not
to allow Indian males from other pueblos to come into
their villages unless they had the lieutenant's permission. There being no further business to discuss,
Leturiondo ended his inspection of the pueblo.[29]  On
January 2, 1678, he quickly conducted an inspection of

---

[29] [Auto to assemble the inhabitants of San Pedro y
San Pablo de] Patali, December 31, 1677, Stet. Coll. Escrib. de Cam., Leg. 156, pp. 551-552; Auto [San Pedro y
San Pablo de] Patali, December 31, 1677, Stet. Coll. Escrib. de Cam., Leg. 156, pp. 552-553; Wenhold (trans.), "A
17th Century Letter of Gabriel Díaz Vara Calderón," pp. 1-
14; Report of Governor Pablo de Hita Salazar to the King,
August 24, 1675, Geiger, Biographical Dictionary of the
Franciscans, p. 130. The population of the pueblo was
approximately five hundred persons.

San Joseph de Ocuya which was located approximately four leagues northeast of San Pedro. Diego Salvador read the Auto General to the Indians, and they responded that they had nothing to say or declare. Whereupon the Sergeant-Major concluded the pueblo's visitation and traveled to San Juan de Azpalaga.[30]

On January 3, 1678, Diego de Salvador explained the contents of the Auto General to the assembled Indians in San Juan de Azpalaga which was located approximately two leagues southeast of San Joseph. The same day Sergeant-Major Domingo de Leturiondo conducted the pueblo's visita. The Indians made the visitador aware of a debt which the Spanish government owed the village. They asserted that Cacique Alonso, who died, sold to Captain Nicolas de Goyas one hundred arrobas of corn and beans to provide food for the garrison. Captain Goyas had promised to pay Cacique

---

[30]Auto [San Joseph de] Ocuya, January 2, 1678, Stet. Coll. Escrib. de Cam., Leg. 156, p. 554; Wenhold (trans.), "A 17th Century Letter of Gabriel Díaz Vara Calderón," pp. 1-14; Report of Governor Pablo de Hita Salazar to the King, August 24, 1675, Geiger, Biographical Dictionary of the Franciscans, p. 130. The pueblo's population at the time was approximately nine hundred.

Alonso for the food with either a mare or stallion. The debt existed for eight years, and the military had made no effort to pay it. This, however, was not the only unsatisfied debt which the military had incurred in Apalachee. The Indians testified to the Sergeant-Major that Cacique Alonso also had supplied the province lieutenant, Captain Juan Fernández de Florencia, approximately three years earlier with one hundred arrobas of corn. This corn was used to relieve a critical food shortage which had existed at the time at St. Augustine.[31]

Cacique Alonso had died shortly before the visitador arrived to conduct the investigation, and the Indians maintained that it was time for the Spanish government to pay the pueblo for services rendered. The cacique of Culcubi, a nearby village, joined the list of claimants also. He testified that he had sold Captain Juan

---

[31]Auto [to assemble the inhabitants of] San Juan de Azpalaga, January 3, 1678, Stet. Coll. Escrib. de Cam., Leg. 156, p. 555; Auto [de] San Juan de Azpalaga, January 3, 1678, Stet. Coll. Escrib. de Cam., Leg. 156, pp. 555-556. See also Wenhold (trans.), "A 17th Century Letter of Gabriel Díaz Vara Calderón," pp. 1-14; Report of Governor Pablo de Hita Salazar to the King, August 24, 1675, Geiger, Biographical Dictionary of the Franciscans, p. 130. The pueblo's population at the time was approximately eight hundred.

Fernández de Florencia fourteen arrobas of corn and had
received no payment. Two hundred and fourteen arrobas of
food amounted to a considerable quantity, and the
Sergeant-Major reasoned that debts had to be satisfied
if the Spanish government wished to maintain good relations with San Juan and Culcubi. He gave the problem a
good deal of thought and conferred at length with the
Indians about it before reaching a decision. He offered
to repay the debt with female "congas mestizas," and the
Indians accepted this form of payment. The caciques and
principal men presented no other complaints to the visitador, and they acknowledged that they got along rather well
with the Spaniards of the province and the transient
Spaniards who came sometimes from Havana and St. Augustine.
Leturiondo, pleased with this statement, concluded the
visita of the village and departed for San Francisco de
Oconi.[32]

The Indians of San Francisco de Oconi, which was
located approximately one league northeast of San Juan,
had no statement or declaration at all to make to the

---

[32]Auto [de] San Juan de Azpalaga, January 3, 1678,
Stet. Coll. Escrib. de Cam., Leg. 156, p. 556.

Sergeant-Major. Leturiondo concluded swiftly their visita

telling them only that they "guardasen lo que estaba man-

dado en los lugares."[33]

Visitador Leturiondo quickly traveled to the vil-

lage of Santa Cruz de Ychutafun, located apparently close

to San Francisco de Oconi. There on January 6, 1678, the

caciques and principal men testified that Indians from San

Francisco de Oconi hunted illegally, from time to time, on

their game preserves. Since an infringement of a hunting

privilege could precipitate a war between the villages

very easily, the Sergeant-Major issued an order for one

of the principal men of Oconi to appear before him at

Santa Cruz. There, in full view of the caciques and their

vassals Leturiondo informed the principal man that the

Indians of San Francisco de Oconi were not to hunt on the

landed area controlled by Santa Cruz. If they violated

---

[33] [Auto to assemble the inhabitants of San Francisco de] Oconi, January 5, 1678, Stet. Coll. Escrib. de
Cam., Leg. 156, pp. 556-557; Auto [of San Francisco de]
Oconi, January 5, 1678, Stet. Coll. Escrib. de Cam., Leg.
156, p. 557. See also Wenhold (trans.), "A 17th Century
Letter of Gabriel Díaz Vara Calderón," pp. 1-14; Report
of Governor Pablo de Hita Salazar to the King, August 24,
1675, Geiger, Biographical Dictionary of the Franciscans,
p. 130. The population of the village at the time was
approximately two hundred.

this order, he stipulated that they were to receive

punishment. He ordered the Indians to abide by the rules

and regulations that he issued earlier to the other

pueblos and ended the visita of the village.[34]

On the following day, Sergeant-Major Leturiondo

conducted the investigation of Nuestra Señora de la Con-

cepción de Ayubali, located one league southeast of San

Francisco. The Indians there had nothing to declare to

him,[35] and he continued on to inspect San Lorenzo de

Ivitachuco located about one league east of Ayubali. As

---

[34][Auto to assemble the inhabitants of] Santa Cruz
de Ychutafun, January 6, 1678, Stet. Coll. Escrib. de
Cam., Leg. 156, p. 558; Auto Santa Cruz [de Ychutafun],
January 6, 1678, Stet. Coll. Escrib. de Cam., Leg. 156,
p. 558. See also Wenhold (trans.), "A 17th Century Letter of Gabriel Díaz Vara Calderón," pp. 1-14; Report of
Governor Pablo de Hita Salazar to the King, August 24,
1675, Geiger, Biographical Dictionary of the Franciscans.
The population of the village at the time was approximately
seventy.

[35][Auto to assemble the inhabitants of Nuestra
Señora de la Concepción de] Ayubali, January 7, 1678,
Stet. Coll. Escrib. de Cam., Leg. 156, p. 559; Auto [Nues-
tra Señora de la Concepción de] Ayubali, January 7, 1678,
Stet. Coll. Escrib. de Cam., Leg. 156, pp. 559-560. See
also Wenhold (trans.), "A 17th Century Letter of Gabriel
Díaz Vara Calderón," pp. 1-14; Report of Governor Pablo
de Hita Salazar to the King, August 24, 1675, Geiger,
Biographical Dictionary of the Franciscans, p. 130. The
population of the pueblo at the time was approximately
eight hundred.

in Ayubali the Indians had no testimony to offer, so
Leturiondo speedily concluded his investigation there on
January 9, 1678.[36]

The Sergeant-Major traveled from San Lorenzo de
Ivitachuco to "el lugar de los Tocapacas de nación in-
fieles," who lived somewhere on the Basisa River.  He
had to acquire the services of an additional interpreter,
for Diego de Salvador did not speak the language of the
Tocapacas.  Martín Ruíz offered his services to the
Sergeant-Major and he proceeded to conduct the investi-
gation.  Sergeant-Major Leturiondo informed the Tocapacas
that Governor Hita Salazar had ordered him to close the
Canal de Basisa where they lived interspersed with other
Indian groups, and to remove them for fear that the
English "y demas piratas de la mar" would raid the

---

[36] [Auto to assemble the inhabitants of San Lorenzo
de] Ivitachuco, January 9, 1678, Stet. Coll. Escrib. de
Cam., Leg. 156, p. 560; Auto [San Lorenzo de] Ivitachuco,
January 9, 1678, Stet. Coll. Escrib. de Cam., Leg. 156,
pp. 560-561.  See also Wenhold (trans.), "A 17th Century
Letter of Gabriel Díaz Vara Calderón," pp. 1-14; Report
of Governor Pablo de Hita Salazar to the King, August 24,
1675, Geiger, Biographical Dictionary of the Franciscans,
p. 130.  The population of the village at the time was
approximately twelve hundred.

settlements situated near to the Gulf of Mexico. The
Tocapacas discussed among themselves, at length, what the
Sergeant-Major told them. When they did reply, they expressed no complaints or grievances but merely some sentiments which revealed their strong attachment to their new
home.[37] They asserted that they had made themselves useful to their Apalachee neighbors, for they had transported
food and other articles for them in their canoes when they
wanted to ship produce to St. Augustine. The Tocapacas
testified also that they used only part of the canal which
they had gone to some effort to conceal from the sight of
an enemy group which might come to the area. They testified that the main channel of the Canal de Basisa was not
open for navigation, for it was obstructed with trees.
The Tocapacas yielded the point that they risked their
personal safety when they went down to the sea, but asserted in their defense that their trips to the sea were
infrequent.[38]

Accordingly, the Tocapacas requested the visitador

---

[37] Auto Tocapacas Infieles, January 9, 1678, Stet.
Coll. Escrib. de Cam., Leg. 156, pp. 561-563.

[38] Ibid.

to permit them to retain their village location. They

asserted that their continued presence near the Canal de

Basisa served a useful purpose to the Spanish government

as an early warning system against an English attack. To

remove them deprived the province of an excellent observ-

ation system, for the enemy could attack the province be-

fore the Apalachees or the Spanish knew of their pres-

ence.[39]

The Sergeant-Major listened to their representation

attentively, and permitted the Tocapacas to continue to

occupy their pueblo site and to serve as lookouts for

Spain. He asked the Tocapacas why they had not embraced

Christianity as their religion, because he found this dis-

turbing, in view of the fact that they lived in close

proximity of Christian Indians for a number of years.

The Tocapacas pointed out that they were not Christians

because there was no one to instruct them in the tenets

of the Christian faith. They agreed that the Christian

faith was good, for about twenty of their fellow tribes-

men died as Christians and received a Christian burial in

---

[39] Ibid.

the church cemetery at San Lorenzo de Ivitachuco. Encouraged by this information, the Sergeant-Major urged
them to become Christians. He warned of the consequences
that befell those who died as heathens. The Sergeant-
Major assured the Indians that he intended to inform the
Father Provincial at St. Augustine that the Tocapacas had
no priest to instruct them in the fundamentals of Christianity. Leturiondo decided before leaving the Tocapacas
to take a census of this non-Apalachee group. He found
that there were two hundred and forty-eight men, women,
and children. The census was not exact, however, for some
of the Indians were away from the village at the time.
The Sergeant-Major was informed that the Tocapacas had no
cacique and he gave possession of the caciqueship to one
of the village elders whom the pueblo inhabitants supported for the position.[40] Having concluded his inspection of the village, Leturiondo resumed his investigation
of the Apalachee villages.

Domingo de Leturiondo traveled from the Tocapaca
pueblo back to San Lorenzo de Ivitachuco where he prepared

---

[40]Ibid.

a set of orders for Captain Juan Fernández de Florencia to put into operation. First of all he directed him to enforce all of the Autos and Mandatos that he promulgated in the province during the course of the visita. He ordered the province lieutenant to enforce the rule that single and married Indian males not travel from one village to another unless they had his permission. If a cacique violated the rule and received one of the vagabonds, the lieutenant was to collect a fine from him of twelve doeskins or items of comparable value. He permitted one exception to this rule, for he gave permission for the Apalachee Indians to go to the village San Antonio de Bacuqua. Apparently this village suffered from a severe shortage of manpower. Perhaps this was a subtle attempt on the part of the Sergeant-Major to recruit additional manpower for the village.[41]

Secondly, the Sergeant-Major instructed Captain Juan Fernández de Florencia to see that a school existed in all of the Apalachee pueblos, so that the children

---

[41]Auto para remitir al Capitan Juan Fernández de Florencia, [San Lorenzo de] Ivitachuco, January 10, 1678, Stet. Coll. Escrib. de Cam., Leg. 156, pp. 564-565.

might have the opportunity to learn to read and write, for the educational needs of the Indians were not adequate. Also, the lieutenant was to insure that the Indians planted food crops for the teachers and assisted them in every way possible. The Sergeant-Major directed the lieutenant to choose the teachers himself, making absolutely certain that they were individuals of impeccable character for this most important task.[42]

Henceforth, Captain Fernández was to visit all of the villages in the province at least once every four months to keep a close watch on Indian affairs and to correct any problems which developed. The Sergeant-Major stressed the need for the lieutenant to make these periodic inspections, because he did not want the Indians to have to travel to San Luis de Talimali to settle their disputes or to ask for justice in a matter. In every case, the visitador wanted the Indian problems settled with dispatch to preserve as much tranquility as possible in the province. He ordered Captain Fernández also to ascertain whether the Indians had the Spanish Royal Coat

---

[42]Ibid.

of Arms displayed in their churches when he visited them. If he discovered that some churches did not have them, he was to see that the Indians erected them as quickly as possible.[43]

Finally, the Sergeant-Major declared that the Tocapacas and their neighbors did not have to move from the Canal de Basisa, for they played an important role in the defensive system for the province. Neither were they to receive punishment because of their failure to become Christians, for the visitador expected that they would embrace Catholicism when they received an exposure to it. The fact that some of the Tocapacas converted to the faith already appeared to him as a good indication.[44]

Sergeant-Major Domingo de Leturiondo conducted his general inspection of Apalachee between December 22, 1677, and January 10, 1678. During this nineteen day period, the Sergeant-Major visited thirteen villages in the province, three more than Governor Diego de Rebolledo had inspected in 1657. Leturiondo included the additional

---

[43]Ibid.

[44]Ibid.

villages of Nuestra Señora de la Candelaria de la Tama and Santa Cruz de Ychutafun on his itinerary, and he visited also a group of Tocapaca Indians who had settled in the province after the Rebolledo investigation. Possibly Nuestra Señora de la Candelaria de la Tama and Santa Cruz de Ychutafun did not exist when Rebolledo came to Apalachee twenty years earlier.

There was a fundamental difference between the Rebolledo and the Leturiondo visitas. Governor Rebolledo conducted his investigation immediately after the Timucuan rebellion of 1656. His primary purpose apparently was to collect testimony which tended to indict the Franciscans and exonerate the soldiers rather than to gather information about the province and its problems. Suggestive of the governor's predilection is the fact that he included no testimony from Franciscans while in Apalachee. Sergeant-Major Leturiondo, however, came to Apalachee during a time of relative peace not in an effort to protect a vested interest as apparently Rebolledo did but to make a genuine inquiry into all facets of village life.

CHAPTER VIII

SERGEANT-MAJOR DOMINGO DE LETURIONDO'S

VISITA GENERAL OF TIMUCUA,

JANUARY 10-30, 1678

Sergeant-Major Domingo de Leturiondo began the
visita general of Timucua province as soon as he completed
his investigation in Apalachee. He inaugurated the investigation in the pueblo of San Miguel de Asile, located
approximately two leagues southeast of San Lorenzo de
Ivitachuco, on January 10, 1678.[1] At San Miguel de Asile,
visitador Leturiondo promulgated a decree which ordered
all of the caciques and principal men of Timucua province
to assemble on January 15, 1678, in the council house at
San Pedro de Potohiriba which was situated about four

---

[1] Wenhold (trans.), "A 17th Century Letter of
Gabriel Díaz Vara Calderón," pp. 1-14; Mark F. Boyd,
"Spanish Mission Sites in Florida," F.H.Q., XVII (April,
1939), p. 256; Report of Governor Pablo de Hita Salazar
to the King, August 24, 1675, Geiger, Biographical Dictionary of the Franciscans, p. 131. The population of
San Miguel at the time was approximately forty.

leagues southeast of San Miguel. The Auto General informed the caciques and principal men of the topics which
the Sergeant-Major intended to discuss with them. The
visitador indicated that he wanted to explore with the
Indians all factors which related to the welfare of the
church, the crown, the pueblos, and the province.[2]

The following day the visitador ordered the Indians
of San Miguel de Asile to assemble in the council house.
Juan Bautista de la Cruz, the interpreter, explained the
Auto General para la Visita to them, and the Indians in-
dicated that they understood everything expected of them.
The interpreter read the decree a second time, but the
Indians had no complaint or grievance to utter against
Captain Andrés Peréz, the province lieutenant, or the
garrison soldiers who served under his command. And the

---

[2]Auto General Para Junta [San Miguel de] Asile,
January 10, 1678, Stet. Coll. Escrib. de Cam., Leg. 156,
p. 587; Wenhold (trans.), "A 17th Century Letter of
Gabriel Díaz Vara Calderón," pp. 1-14; Boyd, "Spanish
Mission Sites in Florida," F.H.Q., XVII (April, 1936),
p. 257; Report of Governor Pablo de Hita Salazar to the
King, August 24, 1675, Geiger, Biographical Dictionary
of the Franciscans, p. 131. San Pedro had, at the time,
about three hundred individuals.

Indians noted that no civilian Spaniards mistreated them

either.[3]

The cacique of San Miguel revealed that he had a

dispute with the cacique of San Matheo, a neighboring vil-

lage, which necessitated the visitador's meditation.  The

cacique did not relate the nature of the controversy at

the time, preferring instead to discuss the matter when

Leturiondo convened the Junta General in San Pedro de

Potohiriba.  He admitted to the Sergeant-Major that his

village had no educational facilities to teach the chil-

dren how to read and write, and Leturiondo ordered him to

establish one.  Simultaneously, he instructed the Indians

to cultivate food for the teacher, and to assist him in

every possible way.  Leturiondo also directed the village

inhabitants not to permit Indians from other towns to

enter San Miguel unless they carried written permission

from their cacique and the lieutenant of the province.

Any cacique or principal man who violated this rule was

---

[3][Auto to assemble the inhabitants of San Miguel
de] Asile, January 11, 1678, Stet. Coll. Escrib. de Cam.,
Leg. 156, pp. 587-588; Auto [San Miguel de] Asile, January
11, 1678, Stet. Coll. Escrib. de Cam., Leg. 156, pp. 588-
589.

to pay a fine of twelve doeskins.[4]

The Sergeant-Major traveled from San Miguel de Asile to San Matheo de Tolapatafi which was situated approximately two leagues southeast. He assembled the Indians, had the Auto General declared to them, and inspected the pueblo on January 12, 1678. The Indians declared that they had no declaration of grievances to make. Leturiondo told them to follow the rules and regulations that he decreed in San Miguel de Asile, and ended his inspection of the village.[5]

Almost immediately the Sergeant-Major departed for Santa Elena de Machaba, located approximately two leagues northeast of San Matheo. On the following day, the scribe, Lorenzo de la Bora, notified Captain Andres Peréz, the

---

[4]Auto [San Miguel de] Asile, January 11, 1678, Stet. Coll. Escrib. de Cam., Leg. 156, pp. 588-589.

[5][Auto to assemble the inhabitants of] San Matheo [de Tolapatafi], January 12, 1678, Stet. Coll. Escrib. de Cam., Leg. 156, p. 589; Auto San Matheo [de Tolapatafi], January 12, 1678, Stet. Coll. Escrib. de Cam., Leg. 156, p. 590; Wenhold (trans.), "A 17th Century Letter of Gabriel Díaz Vara Calderón," pp. 1-14; Boyd, "Spanish Mission Sites in Florida," F.H.Q., XVII (April, 1936), p. 257; Report of Governor Pablo de Hita Salazar to the King, August 24, 1675, Geiger, Biographical Dictionary of the Franciscans, p. 131. The pueblo, at the time, had a population of approximately three hundred.

province lieutenant, of his suspension from office. The
Indians listened attentively to the reading of the Auto
General, but they had no disputes or differences for the
visitador to settle. Sergeant-Major Leturiondo asked the
Indians if the garrison soldiers mistreated them. Specifically he noted that some of the Franciscans had informed Governor Hita Salazar that such was the case. As
a result, the Governor had written to Captain Juan
Fernández de Florencia, in Apalachee, and to Captain
Andres Peréz, of Timucua, to inform them of the Franciscan charges. The Sergeant-Major encouraged the Indians
to speak out if the Franciscan charges were true, so that
he could take the necessary measures to redress their
grievances. The Indians expressed a degree of concern
when they answered the visitador's question. First of
all, they regretted that these complaints had been delivered to the Governor, for they had no basis in fact.
Secondly, they assured the Sergeant-Major that they did
not need an intermediary, such as a friar, to make complaints in their behalf. They declared that they were
not afraid to go to St. Augustine to see Governor Salazar

if they felt that the occasion warranted such an ex-
cursion.[6]

The caciques and principal men emphasized the fact
that the lieutenant and the soldiers treated them very
well. Not only did the military set an excellent example
of conduct, they furnished also protection for the village
against an enemy incursion. The Indians indicated that
they had an idea as to why the complaint was given to
Governor Salazar. After a successful hunting trip, they
had divided excess venison between the soldiers and the
Franciscans. The fact that the Indians gave meat to the
soldiers displeased the Franciscans, and they scolded the
Timucuans for their action. This Franciscan displeasure,
they concluded, was the basis of the untrue report which

---

[6]Notificación [of the suspension of Captain Andres
Peréz, Santa Elena de] Machaba, January 13, 1678, Stet.
Coll. Escrib. de Cam., Leg. 156, pp. 590-591; Auto [Santa
Elena de] Machaba, January 13, 1678, Stet. Coll. Escrib.
de Cam., Leg. 156, p. 592; Wenhold (trans.), "A 17th
Century Letter of Gabriel Díaz Vara Calderón," pp. 1-14;
Boyd, "Spanish Mission Sites in Florida," F.H.Q., XVII
(April, 1939), p. 257; Report of Governor Pablo de Hita
Salazar to the King, August 24, 1675, Geiger, Biographi-
cal Dictionary of the Franciscans, p. 131. The popula-
tion of the pueblo at the time was approximately three
hundred.

reached Governor Salazar.[7]

Satisfied with this testimony, the Sergeant-Major stipulated that an Indian from another village, if he came to their town, had to depart from it after two days unless he had legitimate reasons for remaining longer. Neither was an Indian to relocate in another village without the permission of his cacique and the lieutenant of the province. The cacique or principal man, Leturiondo said, had to pay a fine if they contravened these regulations. As in all of the pueblos that he visited, the Sergeant-Major directed the Indians to establish a school for the children and to furnish the teacher any assistance that he required. The visitador told the Indians that they had to stop using Cuino (apparently some sort of herb) because it harmed their bodies and its use contradicted the teachings of the Catholic Church.[8] Having no other matters to discuss or to rule upon, Leturiondo concluded the village's visita and traveled to San Pedro de Potohiriba.

On January 15, 1678, all of the caciques and

---

[7]Auto [Santa Elena de] Machaba, January 13, 1678, Stet. Coll. Escrib. de Cam., Leg. 156, pp. 592-593.

[8]Ibid.

principal men of Timucua gathered in the council house of
San Pedro de Potohiriba to conform to Leturiondo's order.
The Sergeant-Major asked them if they had any statements
to make about the government and customs of the province.
Also, he inquired whether any dispute existed over possession rights to cacicados or land. He made it abun-
dantly clear that he wanted to get a full account about
everything in the province which disturbed the Indians
and affected the peace of the area. The caciques and
principal men, however, had no testimony to give. The
cacique of San Miguel de Asile, who had deferred regis-
tering his complaint against the cacique of San Matheo
de Tolapatafi until the Junta General convened, informed
the visitador that he had settled his dispute with the
San Matheo cacique. He declined, however, to comment on
the nature of the disagreement.[9]

Pleased that the caciques had settled their disagreement themselves, the Sergeant-Major turned his attention to a very controversial matter, the Indian ball

_____

[9] [Junta General] San Pedro de Potohiriba, January
15, 1678, Stet. Coll. Escrib. de Cam., Leg. 156, pp. 594-
596.

game. He informed the caciques and principal men that he thought it was for their best interest to discontinue the sport. Leturiondo explained that he had suppressed the game in Apalachee province because it was too dangerous and certain aspects of it appeared offensive to Christian teachings. Since the game was so bad in Apalachee, Leturiondo concluded that the ball game in Timucua was equally bad. The Sergeant-Major's comments disconcerted the Indians, and they rose to defend their game, a course of action which the Apalachees had not taken. The caciques and principal men implored Leturiondo not to suppress the ball game in the province, for they had few games or sports with which to amuse themselves. The Sergeant-Major listened to their request but did not rule favorably on it. He noted instead that the Timucuans had a greater obligation to portray themselves as law-abiding and cooperative people, for they had been Christians longer than the Apalachees. If he permitted the Timucuan ball game to exist, then the Apalachees had every reason to request permission to resume their game. As a result, nothing but discord and animosity would prevail in the province.[10]

The Timucuan caciques and principal men did not yield the point easily to the visitador. They requested permission to keep the game, and to support their petition, they testified that their sport was a clean one and did not have the abuses of the Apalachee group. If it were dangerous and offensive to God, then the Sergeant-Major had no other recourse but to suppress it. However, since there were no abuses in it, he should not prohibit them from playing the ball game. Finally, Leturiondo, tired of the discussion, proposed to the Timucuans that they present their case to Governor Hita Salazar, the Reverend Father Provincial, and to the Señor Vicario at St. Augustine. In the meantime, the Sergeant-Major suppressed the game and they were not to resume playing it until the lieutenant of the province said that the authorities had ruled favorably.[11]

Leturiondo asked if any of the caciques, especially

---

[10] Ibid.

[11] Ibid.

a minor cacique, wished to obtain a cacicado of his own.
Specifically, he mentioned an area which he referred to
as Hivitanayo which was located approximately twenty-one
and one-half leagues west of St. Augustine. The Sergeant-
Major was anxious to settle this place because it was on
the route from St. Augustine to Apalachee and could serve
as a way station for soldiers, priests, and travelers.
None of the caciques expressed, at the time, any interest
in accepting the visitador's offer. Virtually all of the
caciques declared that Hivitanayo was too far away to move
their families and possessions. Also they did not have
sufficient provisions to sustain them during the first
critical year. Failing to secure offers to resettle
Hivitanayo, the Sergeant-Major adjourned the Junta
General.[12] Leturiondo was on the verge of leaving San

---

[12]Hivitanayo was located approximately half-way
between San Francisco de Potano and San Diego de Salamoto.
Since San Diego de Salamoto was ten leagues west of St.
Augustine and San Francisco de Potano was thirty-three
leagues west of the capital city, this places Hivitanayo
approximately twenty-one and one-half leagues from St.
Augustine. See Wenhold (trans.), "A 17th Century Letter
of Gabriel Díaz Vara Calderón," pp. 1-14; Boyd, "Spanish
Mission Sites in Florida," F.H.Q., XVII (April, 1939), p.
257; [Junta General] San Pedro Potohiriba, January 15,
1678, Stet. Coll. Escrib. de Cam., Leg. 156, p. 596.

Pedro when Cacique Antonio, a minor cacique of San Matheo
de Tolapatafi, requested permission to take a group of
Indians to resettle Hivitanayo. The cacique indicated
his willingness, in spite of the fact that there were impediments, to settle the area and to carry his parents
and eight other families with him. The families were to
come from San Pedro de Potohiriba, Santa Elena de Machava,
and San Matheo de Tolapatafi. Cacique Antonio asked the
visitador to help the Indians to move their food and other
supplies to Hivitanayo. He requested also of the
Sergeant-Major some axes which the Indians intended to
use to open a Royal Highway and to clear fields around
the village site for crops. The prospect of settling
Hivitanayo so quickly pleased the Sergeant-Major, and he
determined to assist Cacique Antonio and the others as
much as possible.[13]

Immediately, Leturiondo dispatched orders to Captain Juan Fernández de Florencia and Captain Andres Peréz,
directing them to secure the services of the Tocapacas in

---

[13] [Request of Cacique Antonio] San Pedro [de Poto-
hiriba], January 16, 1678, Stet. Coll. Escrib. de Cam.,
Leg. 156, pp. 598-599.

transporting the Indians food and baggage by canal to a landing place on the Rio de San Martín. Captain Andres Peréz was to secure horses from the cacique of Santa Fé and carry the food and baggage from the landing place to Hivitanayo. Also, the Sergeant-Major directed Peréz to send two soldiers along as escorts for the Indians. Leturiondo assured Cacique Antonio that he intended to inform Governor Salazar that the Indians needed axes and other agricultural implements. The Sergeant-Major conferred the possession rights of Hivitanayo on Cacique Antonio and his followers as their personal possession, and to insure that the population of Hivitanayo increased quickly, the visitador decreed that none of the Indians were to move away from the pueblo for a number of years. Cacique Antonio asked the Sergeant-Major to supply the village with a priest, but Leturiondo regretfully informed him that Florida experienced a shortage of religious personnel at the time. However, he told the cacique that a group of Franciscans were expected to arrive shortly at St. Augustine. Hopefully, the Reverend Father Provincial would send one of them to care for their spiritual needs.[14]

Sergeant-Major Domingo de Leturiondo departed from San Pedro de Potohiriba and traveled to San Juan de Guacara, which was located approximately ten leagues southeast of San Pedro. On January 17, 1678, the interpreter explained the Auto General to the assembled Indians and the visitador conducted the inspection of the village the same day. The natives of San Juan quickly admitted that they had no complaints to present against the soldiers, but they did have a request to make of Leturiondo. They asked for a canoe to use as a ferry, for their village was situated in close proximity to the San Juan de Guacara or Suwannee River. As such, the pueblo's location constituted a link in the Camino Real westward from St. Augustine, and the villagers operated a ferry service for travelers who passed through the area. Apparently ill luck had befallen the Indians also, for they asked the Sergeant-Major to provide them with some food. They pointed out that they worked very hard to transport people across the river, in spite of the fact

---

[14]Ibid.

that they did not always have sufficient food to satisfy

their needs.  Because of the hard work and inadequate

food, most of the able-bodied Indians had abandoned the

village and there only remained approximately twenty of

the original population.  The Sergeant-Major took cogni-

zance of the situation, and assured the Indians that he

intended to present their entreaty to Governor Salazar to

secure relief for them.[15]

The visita team journeyed from San Juan de Guacara

to Santa Cruz de Tarihica, located approximately seven

leagues southeast of San Juan.  Bautista explained the

Auto General, but the Indians had no statement or griev-

ance to make.  Leturiondo concluded the village's inspec-

tion[16] and journeyed immediately to Santa Catalina de

---

[15] [Auto to assemble the inhabitants of San Juan de] Guacara, January 17, 1678, Stet. Coll. Escrib. de Cam., Leg. 156, p. 600; Auto [San Juan de] Guacara, January 17, 1678, Stet. Coll. Escrib. de Cam., Leg. 156, pp. 600-601; Wenhold (trans.), "A 17th Century Letter of Gabriel Díaz Vara Calderón," pp. 1-14; Boyd, "Spanish Mission Sites in Florida," F.H.Q., XVII (April, 1939), p. 257; Report of Governor Pablo de Hita Salazar to the King, August 24, 1675, Geiger, Biographical Dictionary of the Franciscans, p. 131.  The population of the pueblo at the time was approximately eighty.

[16] [Auto to assemble the inhabitants of Santa Cruz de Tarihica], January 18, 1678, Stet. Coll. Escrib. de

Ahoica, located approximately three leagues east of Santa
Cruz. The Sergeant-Major, the following day, conducted
his investigation of the village, but the caciques and
principal men had no pressing problems which required his
attention. They did reveal, however, that the padre who
lived in their village prohibited their ceremonial dances
from time to time. They deemed this as unfair treatment
on the part of the priest, for their dances were ancient
customs. They pointed out that other governors, visita-
dores, and Reverend Father Provincials had permitted them
to dance "bailes licitos" while prohibiting, at the same
time, dances which they considered offensive to Christian
teachings. The Sergeant-Major heard the declaration, and
agreed that the Indians had every right to perform "los
bailes licitos." Furthermore, he stipulated that the

---

Cam., Leg. 156, p. 601; Auto, Santa Cruz de Tarihica,
January 18, 1678, Stet. Coll. Escrib. de Cam., Leg. 156,
p. 602; Wenhold (trans.), "A 17th Century Letter of
Gabriel Díaz Vara Calderón," pp. 1-14; Boyd, "Spanish
Mission Sites in Florida," F.H.Q., XVII (April, 1939), p.
257; Report of Governor Pablo de Hita Salazar to the King,
August 24, 1675, Geiger, Biographical Dictionary of the
Franciscans, p. 131. The village population, at the time,
was approximately eighty.

Father was not to impede the exercise of legitimate ceremonial customs.[17]

After the Indians had delivered their grievance
about dancing, Cacique Lucas informed the Sergeant-Major
of an agreement which he contracted with an Indian named
Nicolas Suarez. He and Suarez had decided to establish
a cattle ranch between Santa Catalina de Ahoica and the
deserted village of Ahoica located about three leagues
away. Lucas testified that he and Nicolas Suarez owned
the property where they proposed to establish the ranch,
and that the proposed cattle ranch presented no threat to
the crops of neighboring villages. Accordingly, he asked
the Sergeant-Major for permission to undertake the enterprise. The cattle farm proposal interested Leturiondo
very much, for he saw a certain convenience in

---

[17] [Auto to assemble the inhabitants of] Santa
Catalina [de Ahoica], January 18, 1678, Stet. Coll.
Escrib. de Cam., Leg. 156, p. 603; Auto, Santa Catalina
[de Ahoica], January 19, 1678, Stet. Coll. Escrib. de
Cam., Leg. 156, p. 603; Wenhold (trans.), "A 17th Century
Letter of Gabriel Díaz Vara Calderón," pp. 1-14; Boyd,
"Spanish Mission Sites in Florida," F.H.Q., XVII (April,
1939), p. 257; Report of Governor Pablo de Hita Salazar
to the King, August 24, 1675, Geiger, Biographical Dictionary of the Franciscans, p. 131. The village population, at the time, was about seventy.

establishing a ranch relatively close to St. Augustine.
In times of food shortages at the capital city, and these
occurred with embarrassing frequency, the Spaniards could
obtain provisions from the ranch until the situado arrived. Also, the Indians could sell food to the soldiers
and travelers on the Camino Real, and the cattle ranch
would increase the food supply for the Indians themselves.
With this view in mind, Sergeant-Major Leturiondo gave his
approval for the establishment of the ranch. No other
Indians presented grievances or requests, and the
Sergeant-Major concluded the Visita General of Santa
Catalina de Ahoica.[18]

Domingo de Leturiondo traveled from Santa Catalina
de Ahoica to Santa Fé, located about twelve leagues southeast. The Indians of this pueblo had nothing but the
highest kind of praise for Captain Andres Peréz, the province lieutenant, who maintained his headquarters here.
They testified that he and the soldiers, who served under
him, treated them fairly. Since they had no complaints,
the Sergeant-Major ended the visita general of the village

---

[18]Auto, Santa Catalina [de Ahoica], January 19,
1678, Stet. Coll. Escrib. de Cam., Leg. 156, pp. 603-604.

and traveled about three leagues due south to reach the
village, San Francisco de Potano.[19]

On January 24, 1678, the Indians assembled to hear
Juan Bautista de la Cruz explain the contents of the Auto
General. The Indians had no statements to make, so the
Sergeant-Major turned to consider a petition to relocate
their village. Bartólome Francisco, a native of San
Francisco, had traveled to St. Augustine in November,
1677, where he presented the petition to the officials
of the Real Hacienda. There, he informed the officials
that the cacica of San Francisco de Potano was his wife,
and that he came to the capital city to represent her.
Francisco indicated that the cacica and her vassals desired to move from San Francisco de Potano to Hivitanayo,
an unpopulated village site situated half-way between the

---

[19] [Auto to assemble the inhabitants of] Santa Fé,
January 22, 1678, Stet. Coll. Escrib. de Cam., Leg. 156,
pp. 604-605, Auto, Santa Fé, January 23, 1678, Stet. Coll.
Escrib. de Cam., Leg. 156, p. 605; Wenhold (trans.), "A
17th Century Letter of Gabriel Díaz Vara Calderón," pp.
1-14; Boyd, "Spanish Mission Sites in Florida," F.H.Q.,
XVII (April, 1939), p. 257; Report of Governor Pablo de
Hita Salazar to the King, August 24, 1675, Geiger, Biographical Dictionary of the Franciscans, p. 131. The
village population, at the time, was about one hundred
and ten persons.

Rio de Salamoto (St. Johns) and Santa Fé, in an effort to acquire more fertile agricultural plots.[20]

The officials of the Real Hacienda considered his petition carefully. They pointed out that Bartólome Francisco's wife, who was a cacica in San Francisco de Potano, did not have the authority to remove the inhabitants to settle Hivitanayo. Instead, the Indians of San Francisco were subjects of the cacica of Santa Aña, apparently a village located close-by. The royal officials refused permission for the natives of San Francisco de Potano to change their location without the assent of the cacica of Santa Aña. However, the St. Augustine authorities stipulated that if the cacica of Santa Aña posed no objections to a village relocation that the Spanish government saw no reason to thwart the intent of the

---

[20] [Auto to assemble the inhabitants of] San Francisco [de] Potano, January 24, 1678, Stet. Coll. Escrib. de Cam., Leg. 156, p. 606; [Petition of Bartólome Francisco], November 3, 1677, St. Augustine, Stet. Coll. Escrib. de Cam., Leg. 156, p. 607; Wenhold (trans.), "A 17th Century Letter of Gabriel Díaz Vara Calderón," pp. 1-14; Boyd, "Spanish Mission Sites in Florida," F.H.Q., XVII (April, 1939), p. 257; Report of Governor Pablo de Hita Salazar to the King, August 24, 1675, Geiger, Biographical Dictionary of the Franciscans, p. 131. The population of the village at the time was about sixty persons.

villages. Two additional factors had to be determined,
however, if the Indians decided to relocate. The proposed
site had to be sufficiently large to support them, and
there had to be a large number of Indians who wanted to
move to insure an adequate defensive system. The Real
Hacienda members suggested, as an alternative measure,
the possibility of resettlement in close proximity to
Santa Fé. In any event, the fate of the move depended
on the decision of cacica of Santa Aña. Governor Hita
Salazar agreed with the decision which the Real Hacienda
reached, and he promulgated it in an official decree.
There the matter lay when Leturiondo arrived at San Francisco.[21]

Bartólome asked the Sergeant-Major to permit the
Indians to remove themselves from San Francisco de Potano
and to establish themselves at Hivitanayo. Leturiondo
asked the Indians for their opinion of Francisco's request. The cacica and the principal men disapproved of

---

[21][Decision of the Real Hacienda], St. Augustine,
November 6, 1677, Stet. Coll. Escrib. de Cam., Leg. 156,
pp. 607-608; [Decree of Governor Salazar], St. Augustine,
November 6, 1677, Stet. Coll. Escrib. de Cam., Leg. 156,
p. 608.

the idea. Once before, they had attempted to relocate
their village site, but with unfortunate results. Many
of the villagers, unsatisfied with the new location, moved
away from the area and went to live in other areas of the
province. To move now, they felt, was to risk a similar
occurrence. Accordingly, the Sergeant-Major ordered
Marcela, cacica of Santa Aña, her principal men, and her
subjects to come to San Francisco, in an effort to settle
the matter. Leturiondo quickly reviewed Bartólome Francisco's petition, the opinion of the officials of the Real
Hacienda, and the decision of Governor Hita Salazar. He
pointed out that in the Junta General in San Pedro de
Potohiriba, on January 15, the San Francisco inhabitants
indicated no desire to relocate themselves at Hivitanayo.
Cacique Antonio of San Matheo de Tolapatafi had wished to
settle the area, and permission had been granted to him.
Leturiondo, however, wanted to know exactly how the cacica
and her people felt about the matter before he made a
final decision. Cacica Marcela and her subjects indicated
immediately that they had no desire to go to Hivitanayo,

and the Sergeant-Major denied the petition.[22]

On the same day, María, the principal cacica of San Francisco, asked the visitador for permission to renounce her position. She also requested the Sergeant-Major to bestow her authority in the village on her son, Miguel. The cacica declared that her son was of age, and had sufficient experience to enable him to assume the direction of tribal affairs. María noted that no one forced her to abdicate the position, but that she did it of her own free will. In spite of her testimony, Leturiondo decided to discuss the matter with her enijas, principal men, and vassals. They agreed that she surrendered her cacicaship voluntarily, and the Sergeant-Major, satisfied with their testimony, conferred the caciqueship on Miguel. Subsequently, the Indians installed him with the customary tribal ceremonies incident to such an occasion.[23]

January 29, 1678, Sergeant-Major Domingo de Leturiondo arrived in the pueblo, San Diego de Salamoto, only ten leagues away from St. Augustine and the last

[22]Auto [San Francisco de Potano], January 24, 1678, Stet. Coll. Escrib. de Cam., Leg. 156, p. 608.

[23]Ibid., p. 609.

Indian village he was to inspect. The inhabitants of San
Diego and those of several small villages in the immediate
vicinity gathered in the council house. Juan Bautista de
la Cruz, the interpreter, explained the Auto General, and
the visitador conducted his investigation the following
day. The Indians testified that the lieutenant of the
province and his subordinates treated them well, and that
no disputes or disagreements existed among the inhabitants. However, the Indians made the inspector aware of
a problem in the ferry service which they operated on the
St. Johns River. The Indians complained to the Sergeant-
Major that the work which they had to do on the river was
excessive. Not only was the river very wide at this
point, but there was not sufficient manpower in the village to operate the boats, for many of the former workers
in the transport operation had fled from the pueblo to
escape the hard work. Accordingly, the cacique asked
Leturiondo to send out search parties to locate these individuals and require them to return to Salamoto. Some
had gone to St. Augustine, and he gave Leturiondo a list
of names to use in an effort to identify these fugitives.
In addition, he asked the Sergeant-Major to refuse

permission for anyone to go to St. Augustine to work, for they needed their services on the river.[24]

Upon the conclusion of this request, Doña María, the cacica of Hepo, a nearby village, asked the Sergeant-Major for permission to abdicate her cacicaship. As in the case of Cacica María of San Francisco, she indicated that she surrendered her position voluntarily. She declared that her nephew, Miguel, was the legitimate heir, and requested the visitador to grant him the caciqueship. The Sergeant-Major assented to the cacica's request, and the Indians installed Miguel as the new cacique.[25] When María had concluded her representation, the cacica of Asilepaja, which was located nearby, informed the Sergeant-Major that she had been ill for over five years,

---

[24] [Auto to assemble the inhabitants of San Diego de Salamoto], January 29, 1678, Stet. Coll. Escrib. de Cam., Leg. 156, pp. 612-613; Auto, Salamoto, January 30, 1678, Stet. Coll. Escrib. de Cam., Leg. 156, p. 613; Wenhold (trans.), "A 17th Century Letter of Gabriel Díaz Vara Calderón," pp. 1-14; Boyd, "Spanish Mission Sites in Florida," F.H.Q., XVII (April, 1939), p. 257; Report of Governor Pablo de Hita Salazar to the King, August 24, 1675, Geiger, Biographical Dictionary of the Franciscans, p. 131. The pueblo population at the time was approximately forty.

[25] Auto, Salamoto, January 30, 1678, Stet. Coll. Escrib. de Cam., Leg. 156, pp. 613-614.

and most of the time she was confined to her bed. Apparently, having exhausted all remedies, the cacica requested permission to take "casina" (probably the famous Black Drink) to relieve her suffering. The Sergeant-Major granted her request and stipulated that she was to permit no one other than herself to drink the casina that she brewed.[26] Possibly, the Spaniards tried to prohibit the Black Drink ceremony, because of its association with the ball game and war.

Sergeant-Major Leturiondo issued a decree shortly before his departure which sought to solve San Diego's most important problems. He decreed that because of the small population in the village that all Indians, caciques included, had to lend assistance in the planting and harvesting of the crops. The caciques, apparently unperturbed by this news, agreed to obey the decree. Leturiondo then directed the Indians to construct a larger dwelling to serve as a way station on the east bank of the St. Johns River for the benefit of soldiers and travelers who traveled on the Camino Real. The

---

[26] Ibid.

Sergeant-Major ordered the Indians to gather palm branches, with which to repair the royal road, when they harvested their crops. Leturiondo cautioned the Indians not to abuse the way station when they used it, and he suggested that they had not taken proper care of the old structure. He gave the Corporal stationed in the village strict orders that if anyone damaged the building, Indian or Spaniard, that they had to repair it as good as new.[27] The fact that a Corporal lived at San Diego suggests that the St. Augustine authorities distributed troops in certain villages in the province. San Diego probably merited a military force because of its strategic position on the St. Johns River. Leturiondo does not indicate whether the corporal commanded a group of soldiers or merely acted as a lone observer.

Before returning to St. Augustine, the Sergeant-Major delivered to Captain Andres Perés a series of rules and regulations for the province which he prepared prior to his departure from San Francisco de Potano.

The first regulation, which related to the Timucuan

---

[27]Ibid., pp. 614-615.

ball game, informed Captain Perés that the sport had been prohibited in the province, but that the Indians had submitted a request to the governor and the religious officials at St. Augustine to allow resumption of the sport. Until the St. Augustine authorities decided on their petition, however, they were not to play ball. Secondly, he directed the lieutenant to help Cacique Antonio and his followers develop Hivitanayo into a successful village.[28]

The third order dealt with Indians moving about in the province. In no case was an individual to move from one pueblo to another unless he had a legitimate reason. This, Leturiondo hoped, would make the Indian males more responsible to their jobs and their families. Vagabonds or wandering males were not to enter villages, other than their own, unless they had permission from the province lieutenant and their cacique. Any tribal official who violated this regulation was to be fined twelve doeskins every time he contravened the rule. This regulation pertained to all of the Timucuan pueblos with the exception

---

[28]Auto para que observe lo que se contiene en el el Capitan Andres Peréz theniente de la [provincia] de Timucua, January 26, 1678, Stet. Coll. Escrib. de Cam., Leg. 156, pp. 610-612.

of Hivitanayo. Here the Indians could go, even those who were exiled because of criminal acts. Finally, the lieutenant was to establish schools in villages which lacked them and to secure teachers of good character to teach in them.[29] Having concluded this matter, Leturiondo ended the inspection and returned to St. Augustine.

Sergeant-Major Leturiondo conducted his inspection of Timucua province between January 10, 1678, and January 30, 1678. Altogether, the Sergeant-Major visited ten towns in twenty-one days. Generally, Leturiondo found that the Timucuan problems were essentially the same that he encountered in Apalachee. The Timucua visita did reflect some significant differences. In Apalachee, Leturiondo encountered no instance of the use of drugs such as "cuino" and "casina." He strictly forbade the Timucuans to take "cuino" because he felt that the herb extractive harmed the Indians both physically and morally. Leturiondo made an exception in the case of "casina." He

---

[29] Ibid. See also additional Instructions to Captain Andres Peréz, January 26, 1678, Stet. Coll. Escrib. de Cam., Leg. 156, p. 612.

permitted the cacica of Asilepajo to take the drug for medicinal purposes.

In San Diego de Salamoto, Sergeant-Major Leturiondo dealt realistically with the problems of a village which had experienced a severe loss of manpower. He stipulated that all Indians, regardless of their social or political status, had to lend assistance in the planting and harvesting of the crops. This does not indicate at all that the Sergeant-Major attempted to demean the dignity of the village power structure, rather it is an occasion where economic necessity took precedence over established tradition.

Leturiondo reflected good judgment in the visita of Timucua. He listened to the Indian representations and made wise and judicious decisions. In no instance did the visitador allow the Timucuans to violate established crown and church policies. Yet, he was not inflexible in his judgments. When the Indians presented a case which had reasonable support, he granted their request. Only in the case of the ball game did he defer the final solution to Governor Salazar.

# CHAPTER IX

## CONCLUSIONS

Spanish conquistadors established contact with the
Florida Indians in the sixteenth century and acquired by
mid-century, considerable knowledge of their customs, tra-
ditions, and folk-ways. The Europeans learned a good deal
about the coastal outline and gained some knowledge of the
interior prior to 1565. This knowledge, acquired often at
considerable cost and sacrifice, helped Pedro Menéndez de
Avilés to establish a successful colony at St. Augustine.

The Spaniard who came to Florida, unlike his
English counterpart in the Carolinas, did not attempt to
enslave the Indian. Florida was intended as a defensive
outpost on the "Rim of Christendom," so the Indian was
needed as an ally. Spain built her defensive system
around the presidio, mission, and Indian pueblo. Since
there were not enough soldiers to place garrisons in all
of the provinces, the St. Augustine government counted on
the Franciscans to instill in the Indians loyalty to the

293

king as well as devotion to God.

The military quota for Florida in the seventeenth century was only three hundred and fifty-five men. Much of the time the actual troop strength was far below that figure. As a result, Florida governors concentrated their soldiers in strategically located garrisons. Guale and Timucua had garrisons from the start, but Apalachee had only an observation team, until the Timucuan rebellion in 1656. The governors relied heavily on the Catholic missionaries in keeping the Indians loyal to the crown. Jesuit priests came first to Florida, but they had little success. Franciscan friars replaced the Jesuits and established missions throughout Guale, Apalachee, and Timucua. The Indians revolted on occasion, but the rebellions did not seriously retard the mission program. With a resolute determination the Franciscans returned, after each uprising, to resume their pastoral work. Slowly but surely they reestablished discipline and order among the Indians. Although the military helped sometimes to restore calm to the provinces, the Franciscans preferred not to have soldiers in their doctrinas. The explanation is that the padre and soldier had essentially different goals. Priests concerned themselves with the Indian's spiritual needs, and they worked best in an atmosphere of peace. The soldier, on the other hand, thought primarily in terms of defensive systems. Both the priest and the soldier desired order in the provinces, but the Fathers felt that the presence of soldiers tended to disrupt harmony and create discipline problems. The Franciscans charged that the principal reason behind the Timucuan rebellion of 1656 was the fact that the soldiers forced the Indians to work for them. They had required the Indians to carry food to St. Augustine and had reduced the Timucuans almost to a state of servitude. In spite of the Franciscan protests, Governor Rebolledo stationed a garrison in Apalachee, and the crown did not countermand his decision.

The mission field extended from Port Royal to the Indian River on the Atlantic. To the west the influence of the church extended beyond the Apalachicola River. Brown robed friars busied themselves in scores of villages and towns teaching the gospel of Christ and instructing the neophytes in the catechism. The work was difficult. The Fathers spent long hours learning the difficult Indian languages. Disease, martyrdom, inadequate food and shelter, and a never-ending struggle against unbelievable obstacles took the lives of many sons of St. Francis. Often the Indians changed their village sites and the padre had to move also. Equally difficult was the fact that some of the precepts which the Father taught, contradicted and condemned ancient tribal customs such as certain ceremonial dances and the ball game.

The Franciscans prohibited all ceremonial dances which they felt were lewd or which reflected heathen characteristics. And they felt equally strong about the ball game. The manner in which the players decorated their bodies and the animal noises they made when playing reflected more of "el Diablo" than the finer elements of Christian morality. In addition, the sport was exceedingly rough. Sometimes, in fact, the Indians substituted the ball game for war with about the same results. The Indians did not always accept these restrictions easily, and they protested the Franciscan actions to the civil authorities who visited their villages. Usually, however, the St. Augustine government upheld the friars.

The Spanish governors maintained, as a rule,

constant interest in the general welfare of the Indian.
They sought to protect the provinces from slave raids by
heathen Indians and after 1670 by the Carolinians.
Spanish forces were stationed at key points such as St.
Marks and Santa Catalina in an attempt to prevent foreign
enemies from conducting illegal trade operations. The
presence of the soldier, however, sometimes precipitated
rebellion as happened in Timucua.

In 1656 the Timucuan Indians rose in rebellion.
And the unrest caused by the uprising spread to Apalachee,
but the Apalachees did not join the Timucuan insurgents.
Governor Rebolledo moved quickly to crush the rebellion.
He sent Sergeant-Major Adrian de Cañicares to subdue the
Indians, which he did with severity. Cañicares, who
reasoned that the fault for the revolt lay with the vil-
lage leaders, executed several caciques. Governor
Rebolledo came to Timucua and Apalachee to survey the
situation.

The governor visited both Apalachee and Timucua.
Through the facade of an official inspection, Rebolledo
sought to camouflage the inadequacies of his administration. Accordingly, he apparently collected his evidence

with care so that testimony which tended to criticize him
did not get into the record. He did not interrogate a
single friar. In village after village the Indians, with
monotonous regularity, praised the soldiers and condemned
the Franciscans. The evidence the governor gathered
ranged from the sublime to the ridiculous and reflected
a clumsy attempt on his part to commit duplicity.

The Franciscans contested the governor's findings
at St. Augustine. They also wrote to the Council of the
Indies to protest against Rebolledo. The friars pointed
out that the blame for the rebellion lay with the governor. They asserted that the soldiers had reduced the
Indians to a condition analogous to servitude. Quick to
defend themselves, the friars noted that they complained
to the governor about this unfair treatment, but that he
took no measure to correct it. The Council was impressed
by the friars' statements, and it removed the incompetent
Rebolledo from office. As a result of the rebellion, a
garrison of soldiers was placed in Apalachee where
formerly only an observation team of three individuals
served.

Spanish-Indian relations improved after 1657, and

the mission program regained lost ground. When Bishop
Calderón came to Florida in 1675 he was able to report
the significant results of a dynamic missionary program.
The Bishop administered rites of confirmation to more than
thirteen thousand neophytes. The confirmation figures
possibly were exaggerated, yet they were indicative of a
successful Franciscan effort.

Two years later Governor Hita Salazar ordered a
civil inspection of Guale, Timucua, and Apalachee which
further established the fact that Spanish-Indian relations, at least since 1656, were good.

Governor Salazar chose Antonio de Arguelles to inspect Guale, and Domingo de Leturiondo to conduct the
investigation of Apalachee and Timucua. These investigations differed radically in purpose from the one which
Governor Rebolledo conducted earlier. Arguelles and
Leturiondo made a serious inquiry into the affairs of
each village they visited, and attempted to solve the
problems which they encountered. Rebolledo, on the contrary, tried only to gather evidence which indicted the
Franciscans and exonerated the soldiers.

Basically, neither Arguelles nor Leturiondo

encountered problems which indicated a rift in Spanish-Indian relations. The Indians, with few exceptions, registered no complaints against the soldiers or the Fathers. Primarily, the visitadors concerned themselves with Indian problems such as soil sterility, possession rights to cacicadoes, the relations of Indians to their village leaders, the relation of the Indians to the friars and the military.

When the inspectors encountered problems they issued rules and regulations designed to solve or at least to minimize them. They attempted to insure that the Indians had sufficient food and permitted them to relocate their villages on more favorable sites when soil sterility resulted. Visitador Leturiondo expressed considerable interest in the cattle ranch which Cacique Lucas and Nicolas Suarez proposed to establish near St. Augustine. This enterprise would furnish additional food for the Indians and could relieve critical food shortages at St. Augustine when the subsidy failed, not infrequently, to arrive on schedule. Satisfied that the cattle ranch posed no threat to agricultural areas, Leturiondo gave his approval to the project. In Guale,

Captain Arguelles ordered all of the village caciques to
honor their promise to supply the Santa Catalina garrison
with food. He expressed his distinct displeasure that
this commitment had been observed only by the cacique of
Santa Catalina.

Sometimes the inspectors permitted the village to
relocate or remain for purposes other than the procurement
of food. In Apalachee, Leturiondo encouraged the Indians
who desired to change pueblos to go to San Antonio de
Bacuqua. He secured a group of Timucuans to repopulate
the deserted Hivitanayo village. Also he permitted the
Tocapacas to retain their location on the Canal de Basisa
to serve as an advanced warning system against enemy intrusions from the sea.

In all of the provinces both caciques and cacicas,
on occasion, requested permission to relinquish their
position. Usually the village leaders indicated the heir
apparent. The visitador granted these requests after determining that the nominee had a legitimate claim to the
positions. Sometimes the inspectors encountered a situation where an Indian usurped the caciqueship through
intrigue with the principal men. In these cases, the

visitador validated claims, as best he could, through discussions with all of the village inhabitants. The visitador respected always the Indian process, matrilinear succession, of determining succession to the caciqueship.

Generally, the visitadors did not interfere with
Indian ceremonial customs. In this instance the civil
authorities supported the church. When the Franciscans
became too strict and prohibited all dances, the visitadors overruled them. The inspector strictly ruled against
the use of drugs such as "cuino" and "casina." Leturiondo,
however, permitted one exception in the use of the latter.
He permitted a cacica to take "casina" for medicinal purposes.

Visitador Leturiondo, in particular, expressed a
concern with educational facilities in the Apalachee and
Timucuan villages. His reason is not at all clear, but
may have had a religious basis. Possibly he hoped that
the Indians could acquire sufficient skill to read the
catechism. He ordered the Indians to assist the teacher,
once the village acquired one, by cultivating food for
him. The visitador did not indicate whether the teacher
was lay or religious. Probably, any teaching that took

place was performed by Franciscans.

In Apalachee the question of a government debt to the Indians arose. Military personnel had purchased food from the Indians, but they had not paid for it. Visitador Leturiondo heard the Indian complaint and settled it to their satisfaction.

It became apparent in the Apalachee visita that there was considerable Spanish contact with the province. The number of Spaniards who came to the region from St. Augustine and Havana is not known. The port at St. Marks seems to have experienced a good deal of traffic. Apparently, Spain's enemies were not unaware of potential profit, for English pirates made a successful raid just prior to Leturiondo's arrival in Apalachee.

One incident in the Apalachee visita arouses interest. In the Apalachee campaign against the Chiscas, the province lieutenant, Juan Fernández de Florencia, supplied the Indian arquebusiers with ammunition. In view of the fact that Spain did not usually arm the Indians under her control, this deviation in Florida, from established practice, takes on added significance. It was not apparent in Guale or Timucua that the Indians possessed firearms.  The possibility exists that the lieutenant

loaned the guns to the Indians, but it is just as probable

that the Apalachees owned them.

Throughout the period 1657-1678 one essential theme

emerges in Spanish Florida--the determination to preserve

order.  Spanish governors considered order as essential in

their efforts to maintain the defensive posture of the

area.  They employed three devices in their efforts to

preserve order--presidios, missions, and stable Indian

villages.  Because of inadequate troops the governors

placed increasing emphasis on missionaries and loyal

Indian subjects.  Florida was not a classic case of co-

operation between the civil and the religious authorities.

The Rebolledo visita reflected considerable antagonism

between the two.  The visita which Governor Salazar

ordered revealed apparently a closer degree of coopera-

tion between church and state.  No examples of serious

differences of opinion appeared in the proceedings.

The two visitas of the period, both general in na-

ture, differed radically.  Governor Rebolledo apparently

used his investigation to exonerate his administration of

any blame for the Timucuan rebellion of 1656.  The visita

which Governor Salazar ordered reflected an in-depth attempt to determine the problems which existed in the provinces.  As such, it provided a current appraisal of the assets and the liabilities upon which the governor could, if he chose, make fundamental changes in policy.  It is apparent in the two visitas that the Spaniards in Florida did not enslave the Indians or attempt to eradicate them as did the English in the Carolinas.  Certainly "la Leyenda Negra" is not applicable to Florida.

BIBLIOGRAPHY


Documents:  Manuscript

John B. Stetson Collection, P. K. Yonge Library of Florida
    History.  The Stetson collection resulted from the
    patronage of John Batterson Stetson, who financed
    extensive reproduction of Spanish documents in the
    Archive of the Indies in Seville, Spain, during the
    1920's.  The depression of 1929 brought an end to
    the project.  For a number of years the photostats
    resided in the Library of Congress under a sealed
    loan.  In 1954 the University of Florida acquired
    the collection.

Escribanía de Camara, Legajo 155

        Auto para hacer [la] Vicita General en la provincia
            de Apalachee, January 16, 1657.
        Vicita de San Damían de Cupaica, January 17, 1657.
        Aranzes que se dio a todos los lugares de Apalachee,
            January 17, 1656.
        Vicita del lugar [Santa María] de Bacuqua, January
            19, 1657.
        Vicita del lugar de San Pedro de Patali, January
            19, 1657.
        Vicita del lugar de San Luis [de Xinaica], January
            22, 1657.
        Vicita del lugar de San Juan de Azpalaga, January
            22, 1657.
        Vicita del lugar de San Martín de Tomoli, January
            23, 1657.
        Vicita de San Joseph de Ocuya, February 5, 1657.
        Vicita del lugar de San Francisco de Oconi, Febru-
            ary 6, 1657.
        Vicita del lugar de Santa María de Ayubali, Febru-
            ary 6, 1657.

Vicita del lugar San Lorenzo de Ibitachuco, February 7, 1657.

Vicita del lugar de San Miguel de Asile, February 8, 1657.

Bando que publico por la provincia de Apalachee, February 10, 1657.

Auto, February 13, 1657.

Vicita del lugar de San Pedro [de Potohiriba] y demas caciques de Ustaca [Timucua], February 13, 1657.

Otra Vicita [San Pedro de Potohiriba], February 13, 1657.

Sergeant-Major Adrian de Cañicares to Governor Rebolledo, May 8, 1657.

Sergeant-Major Adrian de Cañicares to Governor Rebolledo, May 21, 1657.

Adjutant Pedro de la Puerta to Governor Rebolledo, July 12, 1657.

Sergeant-Major Adrian de Cañicares to Governor Rebolledo, July 18, 1657.

[Franciscan] Petición [to Governor Rebolledo], August 4, 1657.

[Governor Rebolledo's] Notificación y Repuesta [to the Franciscans], August 5, 1657.

Instrución [from Governor Rebolledo for Apalachee], August 8, 1657.

Exortación y Requerimiento, August 11, 1657.

Petición [of the Father Provincial and the Franciscans to Governor Rebolledo], August 11, 1657.

Repuesta [of Governor Rebolledo to the Franciscan Petición], August 17, 1657.

Petición [of the Father Provincial San Antonio], n. d.

Repuesta [of Governor Rebolledo to the Franciscans], August 19, 1657.

Escribanía de Camara, Legajo 156

Guale Visita

Titulo de 29 de Noviembre [de 1677] por la descargo.

Titulo de Visitador de 6 de Noviembre de 1677.

Nombramiento de Escribano de 29 de Noviembre 1677.

[Escobedo's Acceptance of the Nomination], November 29, 1677.

Auto General de Vicita deste ano de 1677, December 20, 1677.

Vicita del lugar de Santa Catalina, December 21, 1677.

Vicita del lugar de San Joseph de Sapala, December 24, 1677.

Vicita del lugar de Santo Domingo de Asao, December 28, 1677.

Nombramiento de Atequi en los lugares de la Mocama, December 30, 1677.

Aceptación y Juramento, December 30, 1677.

Vicita del lugar de [San Buenaventura] de Ovadalquini, December 31, 1677.

Vicita en el lugar de San Felipe, January 3, 1678.

Vicita del lugar de Santa María de los Yamasis, January 5, 1678.

Vicita [de] San Juan del Puerto, January 8, 1678.

Vicita [de la Natividad de] Nuestra Señora de Guadalupe de Tolomato, January 10, 1678.


Apalachee Visita

Auto [General para la Vicita], December 18, 1677.

Auto [Nomination of the Interpreter], December 19, 1677.

Aceptación y Juramento, December 19, 1677.

Auto, December 20, 1677.

[Junta General, San Martín de] Tomoli, December 22, 1677.

[Auto to assemble the inhabitants of San Martín de] Tomoli, December 24, 1677.

Auto [de San Martín de] Tomoli, December 24, 1677.

[Auto to assemble the inhabitants of Nuestra Señora de la Candelaria de la] Tama, December 24, 1677.

Declaration of Captain Juan de la Roza, December 24, 1677.

Testimony of Captain Antonio Francisco de Herrera, December 24, 1677.

Statements of Captain Juan Fernández de Florencia, Fray Francisco de Medina and Fray Juan de Mercado, December 24, 1677.

Auto [de Nuestra Señora de la Candelaria de la] Tama, December 24, 1677.

[Auto to assemble the inhabitants of] San Luis, December 26, 1677.

Auto, San Luis de Talimali, December 26, 1677.

[San Cosme y San Damían de] Cupaica Auto, December 29, 1677.

[Auto to assemble the inhabitants of San Antonio de] Bacuqua, December 30, 1677.

Auto [de San Antonio de] Bacuqua, December 31, 1677.

[Auto to assemble the inhabitants of San Pedro y San Pablo de] Patali, December 31, 1677.

Auto [San Pedro y San Pablo de] Patali, December 31, 1677.

Auto [San Joseph de] Ocuya, January 2, 1678.

Auto [to assemble the inhabitants of] San Juan de Azpalaga, January 3, 1678.

Auto [de] San Juan de Azpalaga, January 3, 1678.

[Auto to assemble the inhabitants of San Francisco de] Oconi, January 5, 1678.

Auto [of San Francisco de] Oconi, January 5, 1678.

[Auto to assemble the inhabitants of] Santa Cruz de Ychutafun, January 6, 1678.

Auto, Santa Cruz [de Ychutafun], January 6, 1678.

[Auto to assemble the inhabitants of Nuestra Señora de la Concepción de] Ayubali, January 7, 1678.

Auto [Nuestra Señora de la Concepción de] Ayubali, January 7, 1678.

[Auto to assemble the inhabitants of San Lorenzo de] Ivitachuco, January 9, 1678.

Auto [San Lorenzo de] Ivitachuco, January 9, 1678.

Auto Tocapacas Infieles, January 9, 1678.

Auto para remitir al Capitan Juan Fernández de Florencia, [San Lorenzo de] Ivitachuco, January 10, 1678.

Timucua Visita

Auto general para Junta [San Miguel de] Asile,
    January 10, 1678.
[Auto to assemble the inhabitants of San Miguel de]
    Asile, January 11, 1678.
Auto [San Miguel de] Asile, January 11, 1678.
[Auto to assemble the inhabitants of] San Matheo
    [de Tolapatafi], January 12, 1678.
Auto San Matheo [de Tolapatafi], January 12, 1678.
Notificación [of the suspencion of Captain Andres
    Perés, Santa Elena de] Machaba, January 13,
    1678.
Auto [Santa Elena de] Machaba, January 13, 1678.
[Junta General] San Pedro de Potohiriba, January
    15, 1678.
[Request of Cacique Antonio] San Pedro [de Poto-
    hiriba], January 16, 1678.
[Auto to assemble the inhabitants of San Juan de]
    Guacara, January 17, 1678.
Auto, [San Juan de] Guacara, January 17, 1678.
[Auto to assemble the inhabitants of Santa Cruz de
    Tarihica], January 18, 1678.
Auto, Santa Cruz de Tarihica, January 18, 1678.
[Auto to assemble the inhabitants of] Santa Cata-
    lina [de Ahoica], January 18, 1678.
Auto, Santa Catalina [de Ahoica], January 19, 1678.
[Auto to assemble the inhabitants of] Santa Fé,
    January 22, 1678.
Auto, Santa Fé, January 23, 1678.
[Auto to assemble the inhabitants of] San Francisco
    [de] Potano, January 24, 1678.
[Petition of Bartólome Francisco], November 3(?),
    1677.
[Decree of Governor Salazar], November 6, 1677.
[Decision of the Real Hacienda], November 6, 1677.
Auto [San Francisco de Potano], January 24, 1678.
[Auto to assemble the inhabitants of San Diego de
    Salamoto], January 29, 1678.
Auto, Salamoto, January 30, 1678.
Auto para que observe lo que se contiene en el el
    Capitan Andres Peréz theniente de la [pro-
    vincia] de Timucua, January 26, 1678.

[Additional Instructions to Captain Andres Perés], January 26, 1678.

Additional Stetson Documents

Letter from Friar Juan Gomez, March 13, 1657, Archivo General de Indias 54-5-10, Document 73.

Fray Juan Gomez to Father Francisco Martínez, Comisario de la Provincia de Florida, April 4, 1657, Archivo General de Indias 54-5-10, Document 74.

Council of the Indies to the Crown, June 15, 1657, Archivo General de Indias 53-1-6, Document 68.

Council of the Indies to the Crown, July 1, 1657, Archivo General de Indias 54-5-10, Document 75.

Council of the Indies to the Crown, July 7, 1657, Archivo General de Indias 53-1-6, Document 70.

Governor Aranjuiz y Cotes to the Crown, August 8, 1662, Archivo General de Indias 58-2-2, Document 8.

## Printed Documents

Brooks, A. M. The Unwritten History of Old St. Augustine. Copied from the Spanish Archives in Seville, Spain, by Miss A. M. Brooks, and Translated by Mrs. Annie Averette. St. Augustine: 1909.

Rebolledo to the King, October 18, 1657.

Cohen, J. M. (trans.). Bernal Díaz, The Conquest of New Spain. Baltimore: Penquin Books, Reprint, 1965.

Collections of the Georgia Historical Society, Vol. III, Savannah: 1848.

Hawkins, Benjamin. A Sketch of the Creek Country in the Years 1798 and 1799.

Conner, Jeannette Thurber (trans.). Jean Ribaut the Whole and True Discovery of Terra Florida. DeLand: The Florida State Historical Society, 1927.

Conner, Jeannette Thurber (trans.). Pedro Menéndez de
Avilés Adelantado Governor and Captain-General of
Florida, Memorial by Gonzalo Solis de Meras. First
published in La Florida Su Conquista y Colonización
por Pedro Menéndez de Avilés by Eugenio Ruidíaz y
Caravia. Gainesville: University of Florida Press
Reprint, 1964.

Collections of the South Carolina Historical Society. 5
vols. Richmond: William Ellis Jones, Book and Job
Printer, 1897.

  Sir Robert Heath's Patent 5 Charles 1st [30 Oct:
     1629].
  Joseph Dalton to Lord Ashley, June 10, 1670.
  Mr. Mathew's Relation.
  F. O'Sullivan to Lord Ashley.
  H. Woodward to Sir John Yeamans, September 10,
     1670.
  Hilton, William. A True Relation of a Voyage upon
     discovery of part of the Coast of Florida, from
     the Lat. of 31 Deg. to 33 Deg. 45m. North Lat.
     in the ship adventure, William Hilton Commander
     and Commissioner with Captain Anthony Long and
     Peter Fabian set forth by several Gentlemen and
     Merchants of the Island of Barbadoes; sailed
     from Spikes Bay Aug. 10, 1663.
  Hilton to the English Prisoners, September 21,
     1663.
  Arguelles to Hilton, September 22, 1663.
  Hilton to Arguelles, September 23, 1663.
  Arguelles to Hilton, September 23, 1663.
  Hilton to Arguelles, September 24, 1663.
  Hilton to the English Prisoners, September 24,
     1663.
  Woodward, Henry. Discovery, A faithful relation of
     my Westoe voiage begun from ye head of Ashley
     River the tenth of Oct. and finished ye sixth
     of Nov. following.

Corbitt, Julian S. (ed.). Papers Relating to the Navy
During the Spanish War 1585-1587. XI London:
1898.

Davenport, Francis Gardiner (ed.). European Treaties
Bearing on the History of the United States and
Its Dependencies. Vol. II. Washington: Carnegie
Institution, 1929.

Dickinson, Jonathan. Narrative of a Shipwreck in the Gulf
of Florida: Showing God's Protecting Providence,
Man's Surest Help and Defense in Times of Greatest
Difficulty. Burlington: Lexington Press, 1811.

Gallardo, Jose Miguel (trans.). "The Spaniards and the
English Settlement in Charles Town," South Carolina
Historical and Genealogical Magazine, XXXVII (April,
1936), 49-64.

    Don Manuel de Cendoya, Governor of Florida, to the
    Crown, March 24, 1672.
    Don Nicolas Ponce de León to the Queen, July 8,
    1673.

Jameson, J. Franklin (ed.). Spanish Explorers in the
Southern United States, 1528-1543. Original Narra-
tives of American History. New York: Barnes and
Noble Reprint, 1959.

    Hodge, Frederick W. (ed.). The Narrative of Alvar
    Nunez de Vaca.
    Lewis, Theodore H. (ed.). The Narrative of the
    Expedition of Hernando de Soto, by the Gentle-
    man of Elvas.

Kerrigan, Anthony (trans.). Barcia's Chronological History of the Continent of Florida from the Year
1512, in Which Ponce De Leon Discovered Florida,
Until the Year 1722. Gainesville: University of
Florida Press, 1954.

Letter from Joseph Bailey to the English Ambassador in
Spain. The South Carolina Historical and Genealogical Magazine, XVIII (January, 1917), 54-56.

Manuay, Albert C. (ed. and trans.). The History of
Castillo de San Marcos and Fort Matanzas. Wash-
ington: United States Government Printing Office
Reprint, 1955.

Don Francisco de la Guerra y de la Vega to the
Viceroy of New Spain, July 7, 1668, Archivo
General de Indias 58-2-2.

Reding, Katherine (trans. and ed.). "Notes and Documents
Plans for the Colonization and Defense of Apalachee,
1675," Georgia Historical Quarterly, IX (June,
1926), 169-175.

Governor Pablo de Hita y Salazar to the Queen,
June 15, 1675.
Governor Pablo de Hita y Salazar to the King,
June 15, 1675.
Geiger, Maynard. Biographical Dictionary of the
Franciscans in Spanish Florida and Cuba 1528-
1841. Paterson: St. Anthony Guild Press,
1940.
Report of Governor Pablo de Hita Salazar to the
King, August 24, 1675.

Salley, Alexander Samuel, Jr. (ed.). Narratives of Early
Carolina 1650-1708. Original Narratives of Early
American History, J. Fran Klin Jameson (ed.). New
York: Charles Scribner's Sons, 1911.

Sandford, Robert. A Relation of a Voyage on the
Coast of the Province of Carolina, Formerly
Called Florida, in the Continent of the North-
ern America, from Charles River near Cape
Feare, in the County of Clarendon, and the
Lat. of 34 Deg: to Port Royal, in the North
Lat: of 32 Deg: begun 14th June, 1666; Per-
formed by Robert Sandford, Esque, Secretary
and Chiefe Register for the Lords Proprietors
of their County of Clarendon, in the Province
Aforesaid.

Serrano y Sanz, Manuel (ed.). <u>Documentos Historicos de</u>
<u>La Florida y La Luisiana. Siglos XVI al XVIII.</u>
Madrid: Biblioteca de los Americanistas, 1912.

Carta a S. M. de Damían de la Vega Castro y Pardo
Sobre Varios Asuntos de La Florida, August 22,
1639.

Nota de las Misiones de la provincia de la Florida,
establecidos por los Franciscos observantes en
1655, con un convento en la capital a donde se
recogían los misioneros enfermos, sin otros
pueblos de conversion, agregados, y demas que
estaban a cargo de clerigos seculares.

Juan Fernández de Florencia to Governor Pablo de
Hita y Salazar, August 30, 1678.

Wenhold, Lucy L. (trans.). A 17th Century Letter of
Gabriel Díaz Vara Calderón, Bishop of Cuba, De-
scribing the Indians and Indian Missions of
Florida. Washington: Smithsonian Miscellaneous
Collections, Vol. 95, No. 16, 1936.

Books

Arnade, Charles W. <u>Florida on Trial 1593-1602.</u> Coral
Gables: University of Miami Press, 1959.

Bolton, Herbert E. and Ross, Mary. <u>The Debatable Land.</u>
Berkeley: University of California Press, 1925.

Bolton, Herbert E. <u>The Spanish Borderlands.</u> New Haven:
Yale University Press, 1921.

Boyd, Mark F., Smith, Hale G., and Griffin, John W. <u>Here</u>
<u>They Once Stood: The Tragic End of the Apalachee</u>
<u>Missions.</u> Gainesville: University of Florida
Press, 1951.

Bushnell, David I, Jr. <u>Native Villages and Village Sites</u>
<u>East of the Mississippi.</u> Washington: Bureau of
American Ethnology, Bulletin No. 69, 1919.

Chatelaine, Verne Elmo.  The Defenses of Spanish Florida
     1565-1763.  Washington:  Carnegie Institution
     Publications 511, 1914.

Crane, Verner W.  The Southern Frontier 1670-1732.
     Durham:  Duke University Press, 1928.

DeJarnette, David L. and Hansen, Asael T.  The Archaeology
     of the Childresburg Site.  Notes in Anthropology,
     Charles H. Fairbank, editor.  Tallahassee:  The
     Florida State University Press, 1960.

Gannon, Michael V.  The Cross in the Sand; The Early
     Catholic Church in Florida, 1513-1870.  Gaines-
     ville:  University of Florida Press, 1965.

Lanning, John T.  The Spanish Missions of Georgia.  Chapel
     Hill:  University of North Carolina, 1935.

Lewis, Clifford M. and Loomie, Albert J.  The Spanish
     Jesuit Mission in Virginia 1570-1577.  Chapel Hill:
     University of North Carolina Press, 1953.

Lowery, Woodbury.  The Spanish Settlements within the
     Present Limits of the United States 1513-1561.
     Vol. I.  New York:  Russell and Russell, Inc.,
     Reprint, 1959.

Macagowan, Kenneth.  Early Man in the New World.  New
     York:  The Macmillan Company, 1950.

McCrady, Edward.  The History of South Carolina under the
     Proprietory Government 1670-1719.  Vol. I.  New
     York:  The Macmillan Company, 1897.

Mooney, James.  The Swimmer Manuscript:  Cherokee Sacred
     Formular and Medicinal Prescriptions.  Revised,
     Compiled, and Edited by Frans M. Olbrechts.  Wash-
     ington:  Bureau of American Ethnology, Bulletin
     No. 99.

Priestly, Herbert I. Tristán de Luna: Conquistador of the Old South. Glendale: 1936.

Quatterbaum, Paul. The Land Called Chicora: The Carolinas under Spanish Rule with French Intrusions 1520-1670. Gainesville: University of Florida Press, 1956.

Simpson, Lesley Byrd. The Encomienda in New Spain: The Beginning of Spanish Mexico. Berkeley: University of California Press, New Edition, 1950.

Swanton, John R. Aboriginal Culture of the Southeast. Washington: Bureau of American Ethnology, Forty-Second Annual Report, 1928.

_____. Early History of the Creek Indians and their Neighbors. Washington: Bureau of American Ethnology, Bulletin No. 73, 1922.

_____. Religious Beliefs and Medical Practices of the Creek Indians. Washington: Bureau of American Ethnology, Forty-Second Annual Report, 1928.

_____. Social Organization and Social Usages of the Indians of the Creek Confederacy. Washington: Bureau of American Ethnology, Forty-Second Annual Report, 1928.

Willey, Gordon R. and Phillips, Philip. Method and Theory in American Archaeology. Chicago: The University of Chicago Press, 1928.

## Articles

Boyd, Mark F. "Spanish Mission Sites in Florida," Florida Historical Quarterly, XVII (April, 1939), 254-280.

DeJarnette, David L., Kurjack, Edward B., and Cambron, James W. "Stanfield-Worley Bluff Shelter Excavation," Journal of Alabama Archaeology, VII (June, December, 1962), 1-124.

Held, Ray E. "Hernando de Miranda, Governor of Florida 1575-1577," Florida Historical Quarterly, XXVIII (October, 1949), 111-130.

Johnson, J. G. "A Spanish Settlement in Carolina," Georgia Historical Quarterly, VII (December, 1923), 339-345.

_____. "The Spaniards in Northern Georgia during the Sixteenth Century," Georgia Historical Quarterly, IX (June, 1925), 159-168.

_____. "The Yamassee Revolt of 1597 and the Destruction of the Georgia Missions," Georgia Historical Quarterly, VII (March, 1923), 44-53.

Lawson, Katherine S. "Governor Salazar's Wheat Farm Project 1647-1657," Florida Historical Quarterly, XXXIV (January, 1956), 196-200.

McKenzie, Douglas H. "A Summary of the Moundville Phase," Journal of Alabama Archaeology, XII (June, 1966), 1-55.

Ross, Mary. "French Intrusions and Indian Uprisings in Georgia and South Carolina (1577-1580)," Georgia Historical Quarterly, VII (September, 1923), 251-281.

_____. "The French on the Savannah 1605," Georgia Historical Quarterly, VIII (September, 1934), 167-194.

_____. "The Restoration of the Spanish Missions in Georgia, 1598-1606," Georgia Historical Quarterly, X (September, 1926), 171-199.

_____. "The Spanish Settlement of Santa Elena (Port Royal) in 1578," Georgia Historical Quarterly (December, 1925), 352-379.

_____. "With Pardo and Boyano on the Fringes of the Georgia Land," Georgia Historical Quarterly, XIV (December, 1930), 267-285.

Wenhold, Lucy L. "The First Fort of San Marcos de Apala- chee," Florida Historical Quarterly, XXXIV (April, 1956), 301-314.

Wright, Irene A. (trans.). "Spanish Policy Toward Virginia 1606-1612; Jamestown, Ecija, and John Clark of the Mayflower," American Historical Re- view, XXV (April, 1920), 448-479.

Wright, J. Leitch, Jr. "Sixteenth Century English- Spanish Rivalry in La Florida," Florida Historical Quarterly, XXXVIII (April, 1960), 251-281.

APPENDIX

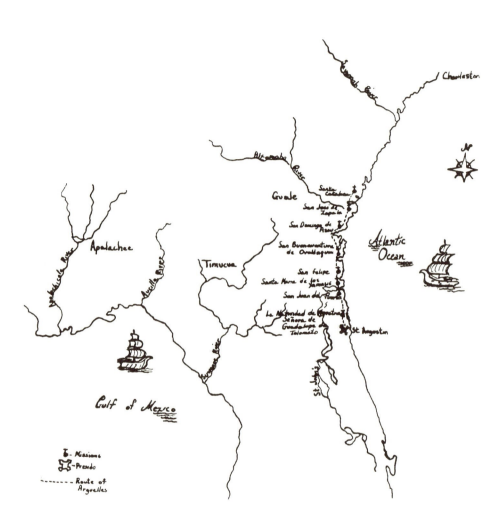

Charleston

Savannah River

Altamaha River

Guale

Santa Catalina

San Jose de Zapala

San Domingo de Asao

San Buenaventura de Ovaldaquini

Timucua

Apalachee

Apalachicola River

Aucilla River

Suwannee River

Atlantic Ocean

San Felipe

Santa Maria de los Yamasee

San Juan del Puerto

La Natividad de Nuestra Señora de Guadalupe de Tolomato

St. Augustin

St. Johns River

Gulf of Mexico

- Missions
- Presidio
- - - - - Route of Arguelles

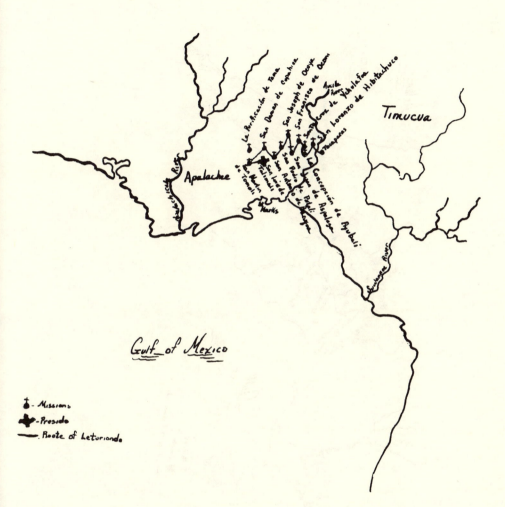

Timucua

Apalachee

La Purission de Tara
San Damas de Capalica
San Joseph de Ocuya
San Francisco de Ocon
Santa Cruz de Ychutafun
San Lorenzo de Hibitachuco

Aucila River

Tomajones

Concepción de Ayubali

Markis

Gulf of Mexico

✝ - Missions
✙ - Presidio
— Route of Leturiondo

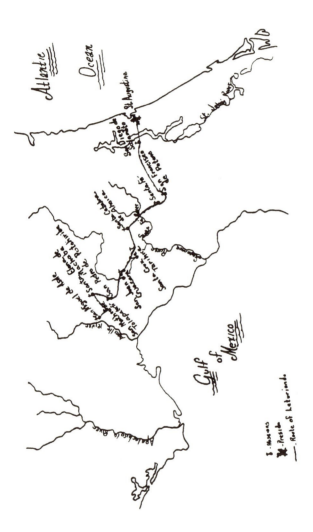